Tales from the General Store:

The Legends of Long Island

Tales from the General Store:
The Legends of Long Island

To Mary —
Enjoy making
your own wonderful
history!

Janet Emily
Demarest

Janet Emily Demarest

Printed in the United States of America.

First Printing: 2014

For information about group sales, licensing for performance or other related questions, please visit www.janetdemarest.com

ISBN: 1500740284
ISBN-13: 978-1500740283

For Tom, Chris and Tim

Table of Contents

Introduction

CHAPTER IV: TALES OF THE AMERICAN REVOLUTION

CHAPTER V: THE SPOOKIEST TALES

Tales from the General Store:
The Legends of Long Island

Introduction

Conklin Barn, Old Bethpage Village Restoration (Author's photo)

Recently I was chatting with a group of fifth graders at Old Bethpage Village Restoration, a 19th Century living history museum in Nassau County, Long Island. As a storyteller who specializes in historic topics, I typically "set the stage", briefly explaining the time and place of the story (for example, Long Island during the American Revolution) and then relate the legend (in this case, a oft-told, very old and probably very tall tale about frozen ducks during one of the coldest winters on record). The children listened intently, laughing at the absurd ending. When the story was over, they argued about the tale's veracity, asking me dozens of questions. After a while, their teacher urged them on to their next destination. The class said goodbye, and began to move along up the dusty road. However, one little girl remained behind. She stood planted in front of me, arms crossed in defiance; her mouth was screwed dubiously up to one side. She eyed me suspiciously.

"Is that a real story?" she demanded.

Yes, Virginia – it is a real story. If it is *true*....well, I wasn't there, so I can't say for certain. But whether or not fowl actually froze during that cold, hard winter is unimportant. It is a legend, a tale that may or may not be true, told over and over for decades, even centuries. The real plight of the ducks is secondary. The legend itself, however - the actual *story* - is quite real and historically significant. Legends and lore, like the actual events they illuminate, have history; this particular fowl tale (sorry) is over two hundred and thirty years old... a long time by Long Island standards.

Today, as we enjoy Jones Beach or head to the Hamptons for a summer weekend, we rarely think of Long Island as having ancient roots. The thought is understandable, as the lion's share of Long Island's growth occurred in the mid-20th Century. Long Island moved rather slowly into the forefront of industry, but it was certainly a place of interest for wealthy businessmen like William K. Vanderbilt II, Otto

H. Kahn and John S. Phipps, who built mansions of extraordinary size and beauty as "summer homes" on Long Island at the turn of the 20th Century. President Theodore Roosevelt made his home at Sagamore Hill in Oyster Bay. Charles Lindbergh took off from Mitchell Field, an airstrip built right on the Hempstead Plains, for the first successful transatlantic flight in 1927. As World War II ended, veterans were invited to come and settle in affordable housing in Levittown; their military background helped contribute to the rise of the aerospace industry on Long Island. The lunar module that landed the first man on the moon in 1969 was designed and developed at Grumman Aerospace in Bethpage. Today, Long Island's world-class research laboratories, such as those in Brookhaven, Stony Brook and Cold Spring Harbor, boast more than a dozen Nobel Prize winners. Modern American history has been, and continues to be, enhanced by Long Island's contributions.

Yet Long Island has a vibrant colonial past that can rival the histories of New England. Our villages of Southold (on the North Fork) and Southampton (on the South) were both settled around 1640, barely twenty years after the Pilgrims landed at Plymouth Rock. Perhaps Salem, Massachusetts is better known than East Hampton for its notorious witch trials, but we had our own frightening and spectacular witch trial in 1657 – some thirty years before

Salem. Lexington, Concord and the Boston Tea Party immediately come to mind when one thinks of the American Revolution, but we, too, had British troops quartering in our homes and farms, providing the backdrop for some of the most harrowing, fascinating and personal experiences of the entire Revolution, and not just Long Island history.

Perhaps it is because of how personal so many of these stories are that they failed to achieve mention in our local history books. After all, these are not tales of famous people involved in history-making events, although occasionally a "celebrity" like P.T. Barnum or Thomas Edison may make a guest appearance. They are, more often than not, anecdotes about perfectly ordinary people who have been involved in extraordinary situations. There are, of course, many such tales in our local history archives, but the stories in this book have been selected for this compilation for three reasons: first, because they are uniquely suited to storytelling; second, they are particularly evocative of the Long Island of centuries ago; and third, they are quite old · every tale in this book dates from before 1899.

Originally these tales were passed orally, with some stories tracing their roots back as far as the mid-1600's. Over the next two hundred years came greater settlement and public education, and the old stories were finally written down and published in earnest in the mid-to-late 1800's. Many, however, reflected the authors' 19th Century modalities and contained confusing language, mystifying references and "inside" jokes that would confound a modern audience. There were also common expressions and philosophies, considered perfectly acceptable in the 1800's, that would make us shudder with political incorrectness today. I have either deleted these

Layton General Store, Old Bethpage Village Restoration
(Author's photo)

entirely, or changed the references to suit a modern audience.

Every storyteller puts his own "spin" on a tale; that is one of the joys of oral storytelling. One does not always know · when the only written record of the tale is a hundred years old - if the particulars of a story are part of the original legend, or made up by the 1890's transcriber of the tale! Therefore, I have included a bibliography at the end of this book, acknowledging a number of those texts, manuscripts and crumbling volumes that have contributed to this work, even abstractly. If you enjoy this book – try reading some of the others!

In my work as an historic storyteller, I often need to straddle the realms of fancy and fact. But surely one would argue folklore and tall stories are in the realm of the fancy! It may be considered strange, then, that no less a world-renowned, research-based, reality-driven historic organization than the Colonial Williamsburg Foundation published a compilation of colonial legends, myths and ghost stories as told by their storytellers, entitled *Witches and Ghosts, Pirates and Thieves, Murder and Mayhem: Scary Tales from Colonial Williamsburg* (compiled by John Hunter, Colonial Williamsburg Foundation, 2007). In its foreword, Rex Ellis, the Vice President of the Historic Area, summed up the value of historical legends and lore by stating:

"The 'future may learn from the past' in a variety of ways. The stories in this book, true or not, were actually told in colonial America...From these stories we learn what colonial citizens valued, feared, lost and loved."

It was this excellent and enjoyable book that inspired me to write down some of our own Long Island legends, in the conversational way they had always been told. Whether the tales are charming folklore or indisputable fact, their value is in how they reveal a deeper sense of past culture and a greater understanding of early Long Islanders' life and times. Besides, reading these stories – especially aloud · is an awful lot of fun!

Much like the vast variety of goods found in a 19th Century general store, you will find in this book a calico assortment of tales and characters: ghosts and witches, pirates and patriots, Native Americans and British soldiers; there are South Shore shipwrecks, North Shore snowstorms, heroes, villains, and some rather extraordinary animals!

It is to remember the quiet patriots and creators of Long Island's past that this book is written. But it is dedicated to the keepers of that past, those who work in public history in museums and historical societies across America, who earnestly and dutifully strive to keep our understanding of the past interesting, genuine, vibrant and alive.

Janet Emily Demarest

It takes a thousand voices to tell
a single story.

- Native American saying

CHAPTER I:
Moving, But Not Exactly Fast

This 1891 real estate map was an unusual marketing tool for the Long Island Rail Road. Despite its best efforts, the struggling company did not turn a profit until 1900 when it was acquired by the Pennsylvania Railroad. (Geographicus Rare Antique Maps)

Maybe because Long Island is so very long (about 120 miles long, but only 20 miles wide), we have always been obsessed with getting from Point A to Point B as quickly as possible. Single horsemen (or in the case of the first story, a single walker) could transverse the Island rather quickly, but once passengers and a carriage were added into the mix, the journey from west to east could take several days. Covered in mud or dust, and shaken to the bone by the uneven roads, passengers rarely arrived

NEW
ARRANGEMENT.

Mail-Stage & **Rail-Road.**

THE U. S. MAIL-STAGE,

Will leave Easthampton, on Monday, Wednesday and Friday, at 5 o'clock, a. m., leave Sag-Harbor at 6 a. m., Bridgehampton at 7 a. m., Southampton at 8 a. m., and pass through the villages of Canoe-Place, Good-Ground and Flanders, to Riverhead, where it will intersect the Boston train of cars at 1 o'clock, for New-York.

FARE from Sag-Harbor to Riverhead $1,00
      from Bridgehampton to Brooklyn   2,27 1-2
      from Southampton to Brooklyn   2,37 1-2

RETURNING:

Passengers must take the accommodation train, which leaves Brooklyn at 9 1-2 o'clock, a. m., to intersect the stage at Riverhead for any of the above named villages.

E. V. HOMAN, Proprietor.

Easthampton, September 22d, 1845.

Corrector Office, Sag-Harbor.

Broadside, Sag Harbor, NY: Corrector Office, 1845
(Courtesy East Hampton Public Library, Long Island Collection)

at their destinations in clean clothes or even a good mood.

Racing became a national pastime in the middle 1800's. Horse racing, dog racing, even cockroach racing (don't ask) quickly became a local obsession. People would place bets on nearly anything that moved. Some years later, realizing that unstructured racing on rural roads were leading to disastrous and deadly accidents, an enormously wealthy Long Island racing enthusiast, William K. Vanderbilt, created the first paved roadway for his Vanderbilt Cup Race. It didn't take long for others to realize that paved roads were the most efficient way to move people as quickly and safely as possible.

Yet, for all of the roads we have built to alleviate delays and move us along, we still get stuck in traffic jams! Dirt roads turned into paved roads, and rails were laid across one end of Long Island to the other, but still the complaints persist...even to this day.

Ah... progress! Here are a few stories about how we Long Islanders began moving forward – just not exactly fast.

Portrait of Stephen Talkhouse, circa 1875, by William Wallace Tooker.
(Photo courtesy of The East Hampton Library, Long Island Collection.)

4

1
The Amazing Stephen Talkhouse

Oh, that Long Island Rail Road! It was a typical lament. Seven hours to get from Brooklyn to Hicksville? Outrageous! It was supposed to take less than three! Seven hours on a steam locomotive? One could walk faster! If it wasn't the dirt from the road or the smell of the smoke or the coal ashes spewing from the locomotive and burning holes into a lady's silk dress, it was mud on the tracks fouling up the switches or entire sections flooded out from the rain. Sometimes was a delay because a big old cow wouldn't move herself off the tracks!

Stephen Talkhouse would never have taken the Long Island Railroad, let me tell you!

Who was Stephen Talkhouse, you ask?

Stephen Talkhouse was a Native American man who, in the middle 1800's, became renowned as the world's fastest *walker*.

Now, before you begin to think that there might be *nothing* more boring, you must remember that Stephen lived in the days before electricity, before any of the devices we consider entertainment today were ever invented. Being the best at something is always exciting, is it not? Well, Stephen Talkhouse was the best at walking. Yes, indeed! Walking!

As fast as you could run, Stephen Talkhouse could walk. He could walk so fast, seemingly without ever getting tired, that he could leave his home in Montauk in the morning, walk twenty-four miles each day to his job as a farmhand in Southampton, do a full day's work and then walk back again to Montauk, just to do it again the next day.

Stephen Taukus (or more commonly, Talkhouse) was born around 1821 in Montauk, Long Island. Even without the impressive ability to walk so quickly, Stephen's life would be remarkable. The direct descendent of the Great Sachem Wyandanch who greeted the first white settlers on Long Island, Stephen would himself eventually become Chief of the Montaukett. He had a fascinating and colorful life, holding a variety of occupations that were unusual even by the hard-working 19th Century standards.

He was born in a wigwam between the Old and New Fireplace Roads in Montauk, and lived there with his mother until he weighed forty pounds; he was then indentured to Colonel William D. Parsons. Being an indentured servant meant that you were effectively sold to another person to work for a period of time – receiving room, board and training but not cash wages – until the terms of the indenture were met. It was a common contract; it enabled a businessman or farmer to have the help of a young, strong worker, and allowed the boy to learn a useful trade. Parsons paid $40 - a dollar a pound – for Stephen, who worked for Parsons until his indenture was finished.

It was said that Talkhouse – tall and thin, with long black hair and a distinctively regal bearing - went out to California during the Gold Rush in 1849. Some references claim he was also once a whaler on a whaling ship. Sometime later, in the 1860's, some sources claim he joined the Union army to fight during the Civil War (supposedly Company G, 29th Connecticut volunteers, a black and Native American infantry division).

But it was his walking prowess that truly made him famous. One story states that Talkhouse once walked from Montauk to Brooklyn - a distance of over 100 miles - in *one day*. But as far-fetched as this claim may be, there is no doubt of his astonishing endurance and speed. He once won a race, walking from Boston to Chicago, against fifty other contestants. He walked so unusually fast, winning contest after contest that he began to get rather famous. Soon circus impresario P.T. Barnum heard of his exploits. Intrigued, Barnum met with Talkhouse and immediately hired him as one of his acts. Stephen Talkhouse worked for P.T Barnum for two years, with Barnum touting him as "The Last King of the Montauks". (He wasn't, but Barnum, ever the showman, thought it made Stephen's act sound more dramatic.) People would pluck down money and line up to race Stephen. Stephen always won.

Stephen Talkhouse was quiet and unassuming, popular among both whites and Native Americans. Always willing to help, he would often take his neighbors' letters to be mailed and would think nothing of walking the twenty-five miles to deliver Montauk mail into Bridgehampton. For that service he charged twenty-five cents. Mighty decent of him!

Boy, could he go! Local legend claims that one rainy day, a neighbor struggling on the road with his horse and buggy saw Stephen walking, as quickly as ever, in the downpour on the side of the muddy road. The man called out, offering him a lift into town. Stephen Talkhouse thanked the neighbor but said no — he was in a rush!

Sadly, he died in 1879 after being chief of the Montaukett tribe for only a little more than a year, and was buried in the Indian graveyard in Montauk. The Indians did not have the same custom we do about putting up gravestones and monuments. But he was so well thought of and respected by the people of Montauk that they felt he should be honored in some way. The townspeople erected a small monument to him in Indian Fields graveyard, the only monument there, a testament to a quiet but extraordinary man. You can still see it there today.

For years afterwards, whenever children asked to be driven in the horse and buggy to get to a friend's house, East End parents told them to "Walk like Stephen Talkhouse!"

2

The Legend of "Mile-A-Minute" Murphy

Delays on the Long Island Railroad have been part of the railroad experience since it was built here in 1834. It was, however, precisely because of how bad the Long Island Railroad's timetable was that Long Islanders observed one of the most prodigious displays of human endurance ever witnessed! It was June, 1899 - and this incredible human being — who could race faster than a speeding locomotive! - was Charles "Mile-A-Minute" Murphy!

But we're getting ahead of ourselves. Murphy's story actually starts with a bicycle.

After the recent unpleasantness of the Civil War, there was a burst of progress, and many new inventions were patented to make people's lives easier. For the first time ever, people didn't have to spend three days doing laundry or harvesting fields by hand. This was something new - leisure time, for the first time ever in their lives! Many people enjoyed that free time by riding bicycles, and they rode them everywhere. A charming Sunday afternoon excursion might involve taking one's sweetheart bicycling along Merrick Road, then stopping at a grassy spot to have a picnic. Merrick Road was a favorite place of many to ride, as it had the distinction of being perfectly flat from beginning to end — ideal for bicycle riding!

Charles "Mile-A-Minute" Murphy
Photo from a booklet published by Charles Murphy around 1915.
(PD-1923)

Charles Murphy was the quintessential 1890's "chap", a dapper young man with an elegant handlebar moustache and puffy mutton-chop sideburns. He proudly wore a blue cycling suit that fit close to his lean body. He made quite a picture, with his cycling suit and his little striped cap, and he would often tip his cap to all of the young ladies as he rode by. At least, when his wife wasn't around!

Murphy was a member of a bicycle club in Brooklyn. Every Sunday, he and his fellow cyclists would ride for miles and miles along Merrick Road, from Brooklyn to Bay Shore and back again.

Charles Murphy was also, as you might imagine, a bit of a show-off. He was known to brag often about how fast he could ride, saying there was not a locomotive that he could not outrace, provided the conditions were controlled. After a number of arguments with his clubmates in Brooklyn, Murphy became determined to prove he was right. However, with a wife and child to care for, Charles Murphy also needed money and dreamed of fame and fortune. One day, Murphy thought of a clever way that he could get both.

The Long Island Rail Road was slow and inconsistent. People complained about it bitterly. The railroad was losing riders, and feared that the new plans to expand the rail network might be in jeopardy. The locomotives could actually speed faster than sixty miles per hour, but the railroad executives realized they needed to not just tell, but actually show people how fast their locomotives could really go in order for people to regain confidence in the Long Island Rail Road's performance. Charles Murphy thought he was just the man to do it.

Murphy met Hal Fullerton, the beleaguered public relations official of the Long Island Rail Road. He asked if he could race their fastest locomotive against his bicycle. They talked for a while, and signed their contract within 48 hours.

A bicycle racing a locomotive! Now, that WAS news! All of the newspapers ran the story. It was all that anyone talked about!

There was a straight run of tracks that had just been laid, running from Farmingdale to Babylon. It was on these new tracks that Charles Murphy planned to race the huge locomotive.

Now, of course there would have to be some things adapted to the race. First, boards were put between the tracks to ensure Murphy had just as smooth a ride as the train did on the rails. But the next refinement was really rather ingenious. In considering speed, Charles Murphy realized that if he were to race the locomotive, he would need to keep right along with it, or he would be wrecked by the powerful air waves created by the lumbering train. He devised a three-sided box to be built on the back of the last railroad car, a sort of "wind shield" to protect him from the displaced air. Today this is called "aerodynamics", but in those days, nobody knew about it. Charles Murphy was a pretty smart fellow!

He also affixed a white strip of paper to the shield right in front of him, so he knew where he had to stay in order to keep centered in the box.

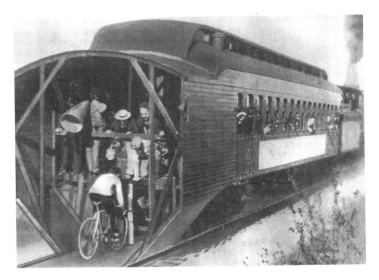

Murphy in the "wind shield"
Photo from a booklet published by Charles Murphy around 1915.
(PD-1923)

It was a beautiful day, June 30, 1899. Charles Murphy kissed his wife and baby, and they nervously rode ahead to the finish line. Murphy shook hands with the Long Island Rail Road officials, posed for photographs, and then got on the back of his bicycle. Murphy's friends were in the last car, there for support and in case anything bad happened. It was planned that the train and the cyclist would get up to speed – the locomotive's best speed, about sixty miles per hour – and then begin the measured mile.

Could a man race a locomotive at sixty miles per hour for an entire minute? Could he really go that fast?

Folks lined up for miles along the race route in order to see "Mile-A-Minute Murphy". Some thought he'd succeed. Others thought he'd get wrecked. Everyone was placing bets on the outcome.

The locomotive blew its whistle. Murphy straightened his hat and focused on the white strip in front of him. The locomotive began to chug away, Murphy peddling right behind. Faster and faster they went, until the locomotive was at full speed. Sixty miles an hour! But the event was only just beginning. Once the measured mile began, Murphy had to maintain that speed for an entire minute.

Well, now! A minute doesn't seem like a long time, unless you are doing something that takes every little ounce of your strength. Murphy took a deep breath. From the corner of his eye he saw the American flag that marked the beginning of the measured mile. It was time! Go, Murphy, go!

Charles Murphy raced faster than he had ever gone. Ten seconds...twenty...nearly half a minute had gone by. He was doing it! Charles Murphy was racing the train! But there was a problem: he had already been pedaling as fast as he could while the train got up to its top speed of sixty miles per hour. That took a minute or two. Now there was still thirty seconds left to go, but by now Murphy was completely exhausted.

Suddenly, the cheers of the crowd turned to screams. Murphy was falling behind! Someone grabbed a megaphone and shouted something to Murphy. He lifted his head to hear – and promptly fell back fifty feet! Oh, no! He knew that if he fell back any more than that, he would get caught up in the train's air currents and be wrecked. He saw defeat was imminent. With amazing determination he refocused on the white strip hanging in the wind shield and began to pump the pedals as fast as he could. Fast! Faster! Super-human fast! He heard the screams from the spectators turn to cheers.

Go, Murphy, GO!!!

From the corner of his eye he saw the American flag waving that showed the end of the measured mile. He laid on the most power he could muster – go, go, GO! - and just as he thought he couldn't possibly pedal any more, he saw the flag streaking by. He did it!

Just then the locomotive slowed down a little too quickly, and Murphy went flying, head over handlebars, crashing into the back of the locomotive. His friends grabbed him and the bicycle, and laid him on a cot in the back of the train car. Murphy was hyperventilating, gasping for air. His blue racing suit was all matted from sweat and full of holes where the hot ashes of the locomotive burned through it.

The train plowed to a stop, and engineer Sam Booth jumped down and raced to the back of the train. He saw Murphy lying still, pale and ashen, and the poor man burst into tears. He thought Charles Murphy was dead!

But just then Murphy sat up, and the two men began to laugh and hug each other. Charles Murphy did it! Hooray! Hooray!

Well, it was all over but for the shouting. Charles Murphy was actually clocked doing the mile in 57.5 seconds, having had to lay on the extra speed to make up for the time he fell back!

For the rest of his life, the famed cyclist was known as "Mile-A-Minute Murphy". Charles Murphy became a bicycle patrolman for the New York City Police Department, and later became the first motorcycle patrolman in New York. And from that day on, what do you think his sergeant in the police station would tell him?

"Go, Murphy! GO!!!"

And that's the tale of Mile-A-Minute Murphy!

3
Thomas Edison and the Black Sands of Quogue

Sometimes even the smartest people do dumb things.

In 1881, 35-year old Thomas Alva Edison, "The Wizard of Menlo Park", had already invented the electric light, an invention which would change the face of the world forever. He was completing the first central electric light power plant in the world, located on Pearl Street in Manhattan, and he and his investors saw the future demand for electricity to be greater than one could ever imagine. To build the dynamos for the power supply Edison needed a lot of iron, and was anxious to find a cheap, convenient supply of ore. Iron ore is not found readily; it had to be mined and separated from the other aspects of the earth where it was found, dirt and sand and other minerals, in order to obtain pure, usable, material. This was no easy process, but there was little alternative. Platinum looked promising but prohibitively expensive, so Edison began to investigate other, less costly, mining and mineral processing techniques. He eventually hit upon iron processing, developing a magnetic ore-separation technique that was patented in 1880. He quickly organized the Edison Ore-Milling Company, backed by the financial investments

Thomas Alva Edison with Phonograph.
Portrait by Matthew Brady in his Washington D.C. studio in April 1878
(Courtesy Library of Congress LC-USZ62-98128)

of speculators. Since this was a venture of Thomas Edison, the investments seemed like a sure bet, with every expectation that the return on their investments would be substantial. All Edison needed was a source of iron ore. Time was marching on; the stock company had been established for a few months already, and still no iron ore source had been found.

One day in 1881, Edison and some friends were fishing off the coast of Long Island, stopping to have lunch at an isolated beach on Quantuck Bay, between Quogue and Westhampton Beach. He was dumbfounded by the color of the beach – it was not a sandy beige, but black! From where he stood at the water's edge, he could see miles and miles of black sand, in layers from one to six inches thick – literally thousands of tons of black sand. Intrigued and hopeful that the black sand contained not just quartz and gravel but magnetite, a black mineral form of iron oxide, he took some of the sand home with him in a bait bucket to test in his lab.

If the black particles in the sand were indeed magnetite, they would be magnetically charged. Eagerly emptying a portion of the black sand onto his work table, Edison took a small magnet and held it over the sand. Instantly the black particles from the sand jumped and attached themselves to the magnet. It was magnetite! Edison was thrilled.

He immediately ordered his assistant to buy

up all the land on the beach, as much of it as he could possibly obtain. He then informed the eager investors from his stock company, and with their capital built a small metal concentrating plant right there on Quantuck Bay beach. Inside the plant he installed the complicated and expensive process he invented to separate the iron particles from the sand by means of strong electric magnets.

Determined to cover all of his bases, he even had a massive loading dock constructed on Quantuck Bay for ocean barges to load the ore.

The ore-separation refinery was ready for business.

But I guess Thomas Alva Edison, arguably the smartest man in the world, wasn't familiar with the kind of land erosion on Long Island's South Shore!

Just before the operation could begin, a tremendous storm came up out of the Atlantic, and every bit of the black sand on the beach in Quogue washed out to sea.

The angry investors pulled out of Edison's ore-separation company, and Edison lost nearly everything he had in the venture. Eventually the plant was sold and turned into a paper processing plant.

The black sands of Quogue have never come back.

4

"The Free Love Colony of Modern Times"

Stephen Pearl Andrews and Josiah Warren (Courtesy Brentwood Public Library)

By looking at the above two gentlemen, one might never imagine that they were what one might consider the original "Flower Children". Do they really look like hippies? Yet these two men ‑ Josiah Warren and Stephen Pearl Andrews, as well as Charles Codman and several other free-thinking, insightful individuals – formed a colony in 1850, in the area that today is known as Brentwood, that was originally – yes, you're reading this right – a commune. Known as "Modern Times", it was an idyllic, utopian vision of society inhabited by individuals who lived by one creed: each person shall mind his own business.

A number of these communities began during the mid-1800's, but none of them were as successful as Modern Times. It was a warm, nurturing, welcoming place, with rules unfettered by the banal laws of 1850's American society. It was developed to support and uphold freedom, make perfect human relationships, abolish jealousy, discontent and greed and eliminate poverty and war. It was to be Paradise.

(And you thought you just lived in Brentwood.)

"Minding one's own business" extended across many cultural boundaries. Marriage in Modern Times was a fluid and somewhat arbitrary institution. If one was considered "tied" to another person, the man and woman involved would each wear a red string around his or her finger. If the relationship was no longer desired, the parties involved would simply untie the string and the marriage was considered annulled.

With such an unusual form of nuptials, it was understandably gauche for anyone to inquire as to who a woman's husband was, or who the father of a particular child was. Things simply were the way they were. Free love, man!

There was no crime – no theft, no lying, no cheating, no jealousy, and no murder – and people lived in a respectful relationship with one another. The honesty of the community can be illustrated by a tale, told over and over for many years, about a lost watch. The story goes that a visiting peddler dropped his expensive gold watch and chain in the street as he was passing through the village. A local resident found the watch and hung it on a nail on the bulletin board outside of the local actors' theater, a popular gathering spot. There it remained for ten days, until the peddler returned to the village and saw his watch hanging there, waiting for its rightful owner, on the town board. Imagine that happening today!

All food was communal, all crops grown were shared. The community planted beautiful cathedral pines, for which the town became known. They even planted apple trees along the road, so that a tired traveler would have something to eat as he passed by.

For ten years, Modern Times was truly a lovely place to live, a utopia that perpetuated the best in people and drew in those who simply preferred to live by their own rules and beliefs. One convert, a Reverend Moncure Daniel Conway, stated that the colony could be found "either by railway or by rainbow". It was said that another nameless person added, "It was closer to the rainbow than to the railroad."

Unfortunately, eventually the newspapers of the day got hold of the story of the unusual town, and began to sensationalize (as was their wont before truth in journalism laws were enacted). Suddenly all sorts of odd-balls, troublemakers and iconoclasts began to arrive at Modern Times in droves. It was, after all, the 1850's! One woman wore only men's clothing. One man came and brought several wives. Another woman insisted on eating only beans and despite the frantic coaxing of her neighbors, refused to take any other nutrition; she died within the year. Yet another man came, and truly scandalized the small town – he was a nudist!

Well! Eventually, it all became too much for the tiny community to bear. The town resettled itself into a more recognizable and conventional society, and renamed itself Brentwood. The utopia that was Modern Times had come to an end.

5
The More Things Change.....

Back in the 1700's, it was common courtesy for people to open their homes to strangers who begged an accommodation or a meal. With greater strides in transportation bringing increasing numbers of people to out-of-the-way communities, this hospitality became an understandably difficult tradition to continue. However, in very rural areas like Montauk and Amagansett, it lasted for quite some time.

Today, as in years past, city folks love to get away from the heat and grime, and spend lazy summer weekends at the beach on the East End. Local merchants do love their visitors, as they provide a measure of affluence for the quiet communities; but the truth of the matter is that sometimes the local residents very quietly whisper among themselves that they can't *wait* until September comes and they can have their roads back to themselves. One really cannot blame them, as a ten minute errand to the market turns into an hour's ordeal in July and August.

This attitude is not due to any mean-spiritedness on the part of the residents. No! In actuality, it has been found to be an inbred sentiment, stemming back more than 150 years, if the following essay is an indication:

"On the beach at Long Beach: a new and popular seaside resort"
Frank Leslie's Illustrated Newspaper, v. 54, August 12, 1882
(Zoom image; PD-1923)

"... now, in place of travelling soberly along, we, by means of railroads and turnpikes, fly rapidly through the island. Now we will meet with hundreds of tourists for pleasure, where we (once) met one ... It was then something of an undertaking to go to Montauk Point – now almost everybody goes there. Then there were few taverns, and in many places none; the inhabitants were delighted to see strangers, and learn from them the news of the world; they were plain and hospitable in their manners, so it was a peculiar pleasure to visit them. Now there are taverns or hotels everywhere, and in the summer they are filled. The people have ceased to offer their hospitalities, except to those with whom they are somewhat acquainted, otherwise from the great influx of strangers they might be much imposed upon..."

Gabriel Furman
Antiquities of Long Island
1840

And so, the more things change, the more they stay the same. Ah...progress!

Illustration from *King Philip*
by John S.C.Abbott, 1857 (PD-1923)

CHAPTER II
Paumonock Tales

Windmill on Gardiners Island
Sketch by Alfred Waud, 1875
(East Hampton Library, Long Island Collection)

One doesn't really think of Long Island as having a history spanning from the time of the earliest settlers to America, but it does. In fact, it was only twenty years after the Pilgrims landed at Plymouth Rock that their progeny and contemporaries travelled across Long Island Sound and established settlements where Southold, East Hampton and Southampton are today. 1640 was a long, long time ago! That gives us plenty of time to gather up some legendary tales, and most of the earliest ones had to do with our first neighbors – the Native American tribes of Long Island.

There were a great many Native Americans who lived here long before the European settlers came into Manhattan and Queens at the end of the 1500's. The Siwanoy were one tribe that resided around the curve of land between Long Island and the Bronx. At the opposite end of the Island, the Puritans from Massachusetts and Connecticut expanded from their original colonies and settled here around 1640. They met another Indian tribe, the Montaukett, and developed a peaceful coexistence with them, as evidenced in the story "The Ransom of Heather Flower".

The Native Americans on Long Island's east end called Long Island "Paumonock". It means "land of tribute" or "fish-shaped land". How can it mean two entirely different things? Well, fact is, it really doesn't. A tribute is a gift, given freely (or sometimes not so freely) to one another. The Indians on Long Island had to give tribute to the powerful Narragansett Indians in Connecticut across the Sound. A typical tribute was a bushel (or many bushels) of fish. So a tribute was often automatically thought of as fish. Paumonock! Fish Land!

The stories that follow have been told and retold for nearly four centuries. They reflect not only the fear and suspicion that came with settling in a new land, but also the bravery, wit and romance that was prized in our earliest settlers' society.

6
The Devil's Belt and the Devil's Stepping Stones

"The Country twenty five miles round New York, drawn by a gentleman from that city. J. Barber, sculp." (zoom image). Map published by W. Hawkes, London, 1776. (Courtesy LOC.gmd/g3804n.ar109601)

Long Island Sound was known as "The Devil's Belt" in the earliest colonial times. It is not clear why the Sound was so nick-named, but it might likely have come from the devilishly deceptive and inconsistent waters off the northern shore of Long Island. Some harbors have deep water, while others are very shallow. Hidden sandbars and rocky shoals are often disguised by high tides that make the waters, especially those closest to Manhattan, treacherous to navigate. Add to this the wicked nor'easters that mark the area, proximity to an onshore area called Hell's Gate, and the reference to the Devil in relation to those islands in an ancient legend (see below), and there is a reasonable explanation why Long Island Sound could have been likened by the earliest seafarers and traders to "The Devil's Belt".

At the furthest western waters of the Sound, on the border of Manhattan (around City Island), there are a number of small islands jutting up from the water, some more visible than others depending on the tide. These treacherous islands have been known by seafarers, as far back as Henry Hudson in 1609, as "The Devil's Stepping-Stones".

A very old Siwanoy Indian legend states that once upon a time, a long, long time ago, Long Island had hundreds of rocks on its shore, but Connecticut had none. One day the Devil himself was chased by the Indians out of Connecticut and pushed back across Long Island Sound. The Devil was frightened by the fearsome braves, and he ran furiously, using the scores of small islands just east of Manhattan as footholds. Once on Long Island, the evil one furiously flung every boulder and rock he could find back across the water at the braves, and although his arm was powerful, his aim was not true. It was from the stones the Devil threw, it was said, hitting everywhere except his targets, that the shores of Connecticut and New England became littered with stone formations.

A little red brick Victorian lighthouse was built around 1875 on the tip of Long Island, in the waters between King's Point in the east and the Throg's Neck Bridge in the west. Christened "Stepping Stones Light", its original light was, appropriately enough for a legendary devil, a steady red beacon.

Stepping Stones Lighthouse (Photo courtesy U.S. Coast Guard)

Illustration from *King Philip*
by John S.C.Abbott, 1857 (PD-1923)

7
The Ransom of Heather Flower

One of our earliest legends is nearly four hundred years ago, and concerns a great battle, a beautiful bride and a bitter rivalry between the chief of the Montaukett, the Great Sachem Wyandanch, and his arch-enemy, Chief Ninigret, who was the leader of the fierce Narragansett tribe in Connecticut. It is also the story of a very special friendship between Wyandanch and one of the first settlers on Long Island, who had the most unusual name of Lion Gardiner. He put his own life in danger to rescue Chief Wyandanch's daughter from the Narragansett tribe, and legend says he was rewarded quite handsomely for it.

We mentioned before that tribute was often bushels of fish. Well, perhaps a common tribute might be fish, but an even better tribute was wampum. And no one had better wampum than the Montaukett of Long Island! The beautiful, chalky white and purple clamshells that littered the beaches of Long Island made the finest and most desirable wampum. It was so prized by the natives, in fact, that when the English settlers came to the East End, they soon realized that their silver and pieces of eight had no value here. They quickly adopted wampum as their currency.

The Indians traded wampum for the things

they were unable to make or get, and the metal pots and utensils of the English were greatly desired. Instead of spending many days cutting the hard burls from trees, hollowing them out, putting coals in them to make a sturdy center and eventually creating a usable wooden pot, they could trade with the English for items that were made of metal, far superior to wood. With the English also came metal weapons, knives and muskets, and Chief Wyandanch quickly understood the value of having these white settlers co-exist peaceably with them on the East End. A favorable trading relationship soon grew into a friendship with the head of the English settlement, Lion Gardiner.

Gardiner founded the first English settlement in New York on the eastern end of Long Island in 1639, having his own home on "The Isle of Wight", a large island he named after his ancestral home (we know it today as Gardiner's Island). A hero of the Pequot War in Connecticut, he was quite familiar with the tribes of Connecticut, especially the Narragansett.

After the Pequot wars, the young Narragansett chief Ninigret was determined to re-establish the Narragansett's preeminence in the area. When Wyandanch began trading and forming relationships with the white settlers, Ninigret realized that his days of controlling the Montaukett were numbered. He wanted to teach Wyandanch a lesson, and began to hatch a plan to destroy his enemy.

Wyandanch had a daughter, his pride and joy. Her name was Momone, or "Heather Flower". She was to be wed to a Shinnecock chief, and there was much rejoicing. It was going to be a grand three-day occasion, and everyone was invited to celebrate the marriage. Women prepared enormous bowls of vegetables and food while larger game roasted. Fermented drinks flowed. Bonfires blazed, drums pounded, people shouted and danced; there were games and shooting contests. Everyone enjoyed the feast!

Montaukett guards were supposed to look out for danger. But they had no idea that during the drumming, the smoke and the noise of the bridal festivities, Narragansett warriors silently rowed across Long Island Sound from Connecticut in war canoes and quietly pulled up on the Montauk shore. They waited in silence until just the right time. Late at night, when the guards were sleepy and vulnerable, the Narragansett warriors jumped up from their hiding places and attacked! There was utter pandemonium! Women were screaming, arrows were flying; Wyandanch was scurried into safety by his guards while the Narragansett killed nearly every brave, including the bridegroom.

The Narragansett swiftly took their war canoes back to Connecticut. The bloody battle was over. But as the shattered remnants of the tribe staggered back, Wyandanch made a horrifying discovery — the Narragansett had taken his daughter!

Wyandanch was beside himself with grief. He needed to get back his daughter, but how? He could not trust Ninigret, and was unwilling to negotiate with him regarding a ransom. It broke his heart to know that Heather Flower would become a slave to Ninigret and his family. But Ninigret did not trust Wyandanch, either, and so negotiations between the two chiefs seemed almost hopeless. How would the talks even begin? But Lion Gardiner, realizing a solution, calmly said to Wyandanch "I'll go", and with that, Gardiner travelled to Connecticut to begin negotiations for Heather Flower's release.

It was a delicate diplomatic effort, one that took much time, patience and skill in negotiation. But eventually, Lion Gardiner succeeded in ransoming Heather Flower. It took *seven years*, but he succeeded. One can only imagine the tears of joy when Heather Flower was reunited with her father at last!

From that point on, Chief Wyandanch called Lion Gardiner "Brother", and rewarded him with giant tracts of land. He made Gardiner the guardian of his son, and stated that after his death, his wife could not make any important decisions on her own without consulting Lion Gardiner first.

There is a happy ending to this story for Heather Flower as well. During the seven years she was held as a slave in the Narragansett tribe, legend claims she met and fell in love with a Pequot brave, who had survived the Pequot massacre and was also being held as a slave. She begged her father to also provide ransom for the young man, and upon his release he and Heather Flower were married. Some legends say that they had a son together, and Heather Flower named him *Wyandanch Lion*.

At The Landing, Gardiner's Island
From "An American Lordship", December 1885, *The Century Illustrated Magazine* by George Parsons Lathrop (PD-1923)

Lake Ronkonkoma (Author's photo)

8
The Mystery of Lake Ronkonkoma

The next story has been a Long Island legend for four hundred years · nearly as long as there has been Long Island history! Some people claim that the Indian woman in the story is Heather Flower – but it seems unlikely that she would have travelled some seventy miles, all the way from Montauk to the middle of Long Island, just to drown herself in a big lake!

This story takes place at Lake Ronkonkoma, a fresh water lake in the middle of Long Island. Some really strange, eerie things are said to happen there, and legends surrounding its mystery have abounded since the late 1600's.

The most common legend states that long, long ago, a beautiful Indian maiden's love, a handsome Indian brave, was killed in battle, and she was heartbroken. Unable to be consoled, she determined to kill herself in order to join with her dead love. To that end she tied heavy rocks around her waist, waded out into the middle of Lake Ronkonkoma, and drowned herself. But it is said that before she died, she uttered a terrible curse! She decreed that she would avenge the death of her beloved brave by taking one male life per year, every year, for as long as the lake had water in it.

Well, Lake Ronkonkoma shows no signs of drying up any time soon. And it is true that there have been drownings – not one a year, as the Indian maiden supposedly said, but a fairly large number of drownings over the years. However, there is often something peculiar about those drownings. Sometimes the bodies are found in Lake Ronkonkoma, true. But sometimes the bodies turn up in Long Island Sound. Sometimes they are even found in the East River by Manhattan!

As if that is not enough, other odd things happen there as well. It is said if you take a boat out into the middle of the lake, you may suddenly hear the voice of a woman calling to you. It is said to be the voice of the Indian maiden. Do not answer! She is calling you to your death!

Many people claim that the lake is bottomless – but if you look deeply into the water, you will see sparkles coming up from the depths of the dark, deep lake. Do not get so intrigued by them that you lean too far over the side of your little boat! For it is said that those who lean out over the water are not pushed out of their boat into the water – they are *pulled* down to their watery grave!

There is no doubt that Lake Ronkonkoma is a beautiful lake, and each year a great many people venture out to enjoy a day on the water. However, many local folks still refuse to go swimming in Lake Ronkonkoma – at least, not until the first drowning of the year occurred. You know... just to be safe!

9
The Incredible Smithtown Bull

The "Incredible Smithtown Bull" may have been a Randall Lineback, like this handsome mature male. An "all-purpose" breed, Randalls were common in New England in the mid-1600's and gave the milk, provided the meat, and did much of the heavy agricultural work. Critically rare, it is now one of the most endangered breeds of cattle in the world. (Photo courtesy of Randall Lineback Breed Association)

Well, there are many stories about the natives and the new settlers... but none of them are quite as real and enduring as the Tale of the Smithtown Bull. Out of all of the Long Island legends, this is the one most people know, even today! It is one of our oldest tales; the legend has been around since the middle 1600's.

If you ride into Smithtown today, you might be surprised to see an enormous statue of a bull there greeting you at the beginning of the town. That is Whisper, the Smithtown Bull – and it is because of Whisper that Smithtown actually became a town.

So here it goes...

People came to America from England as far back as back as the year 1585. After a few unsuccessful attempts, the English finally established a thriving colony in Virginia. Most of these early settlers were unmarried men, adventurers who wanted to make a life for themselves. But just a few years later, there was a different king in England. Because he wanted everyone to worship the way he worshipped, many people got upset and decided to flee the country. These were not adventurers but common people who had very strict religious beliefs, and they were known as Puritans, or Pilgrims. When they came to America, they came with wife and family, and landed north, in New England, eventually establishing the Massachusetts Bay and Connecticut Colonies. They were so strict that they did not even celebrate Christmas! They felt that the best way for survival was for everyone to think and behave the same way, and not be too outrageous. The young, energetic, enthusiastic Richard Smith, who had ideas and plans and ambition and drive, was just too much for the elders of the early colony. They kicked him out.

Did that stop Richard Smith? No! He went across the Sound to Long Island. He looked around and saw a wonderful parcel of land — acres and acres of good land — and determined that he was going to obtain that land and begin to build a town of his own. There was only one problem — the natives who lived on the land refused to sell it to him!

Did that stop Richard Smith? No! He quietly traded with the Indians and watched them carefully. He noticed that they liked to play games, particularly games of chance. So one day, Richard Smith went to speak to the chief, and made him a wager. "You know that parcel of land I've been speaking to you about?" Richard Smith asked. "If I can circle it completely in one day, while riding on the back of a bull, will you sell it to me? If I cannot do it, you can have my bull. What do you think? Do we have a wager?"

The natives laughed hysterically. What fool would make such a wager? The chief agreed, and Smith set the date of the bull-riding wager as June 21. Why June 21? Well, that day is known as the summer solstice — the longest day of the year. Richard Smith was no fool. He knew he needed as much daylight as he could possibly get in order to circle the entire parcel on the back of his bull.

But this was no ordinary bull story, although it may sound so at first! This was the marvelous Whisper, Richard Smith's pet bull.

Richard Smith had an extraordinary relationship with Whisper. He would often jump on Whisper's back and ride him like a horse as they were plowing the fields. Smith was gentle and kind to Whisper, giving him treats and special attention, and Whisper behaved more like a pet dog than a bull. He loved Richard Smith – almost as much as he loved his girlfriend, a little brown cow named Daisy. And Richard Smith knew that wherever Daisy went, Whisper was sure to follow.

The day before the bull-riding wager, June 20, in fact, Richard Smith took Daisy the cow from her pasture and walked her slowly around the entire parcel of land he wanted to gain from the Indians. And as she walked, she did...well, what any cow would naturally be expected to do, now and then. Clever Richard Smith knew Whisper would follow Daisy's irresistible aroma to the ends of the earth. It was in this way that he prepared for the wager the following day.

Finally, the morning of the wager began to dawn. All of the natives gathered to watch as this fool climbed on the back of his bull. They laughed hysterically, placing bets on the outcome. Richard Smith jumped onto Whisper's back. As the sun was beginning to peak over the eastern horizon, with a wave of his hat, he and Whisper took off.

It was a fixing to be a hot day, but they got an early start, with Whisper gleefully following his girlfriend's scent from the day before and looking for Daisy around every corner. By noon-time Richard Smith was pleased to see that he and Whisper had circled more than half the land. He stopped the bull, fed him some grass and water, and took a few minutes to cool off in a little hollow, pulling some bread and cheese out of his sack for a quick lunch. The people of Smithtown are so certain that this happened there, they named a road that runs through the middle of town today "Bread and Cheese Hollow Road." Surely the people of Smithtown would not have named it that if it didn't really happen!

Well, lunch being over, Richard Smith gave Whisper another quick drink of water, climbed again on his back and continued his ride. But the day was getting blisteringly hot, and they travelled slower and slower all afternoon. Richard Smith was distraught; it looked like his wager was lost, and his beloved pet bull, to boot. The sun was going down, and they were still two miles away from the finish line. "Well, old friend," Smith said, reaching over and scratching the bull between his horns at the top of his head. "We gave it our best, and no one can ask for better than that."

But just then, fate intervened! A bee, who had been buzzing around annoying Whisper for some time, settled down on Whisper's flank and stung him right where it hurt! Whisper yelped and took off like a shot! Richard Smith had to hang on for dear life! The big bull literally galloped the last two miles and they made it over the finish line just as the sun was beginning to set. Richard Smith had won his land! Huzzah!

And if you don't believe that part about the bee, go on out of town about two miles – and there you will find a road known as Bee Drive. Surely the people of Smithtown would not have named it that if it were not the exact spot where the bee drove Whisper to hurry back to the finish line!

So that is the amazing story of The Smithtown Bull! If you don't believe me, take a ride out to Smithtown some day and talk to the folks out there. Ask them about Whisper. The people of Smithtown will tell you that this is absolutely a true story.

10
The Blue Point Oyster Rebellion

Blue Point, by the Great South Bay, is known even today for its delicious, succulent oysters. But a peculiarity occurred back in the early 1800's that made the citizens of Brookhaven wonder if the oysters were placed there by God as a test for the residents – or if the shellfish had God-fearing minds of their own.

Legend claims that poor people from all over the area would come to harvest the oysters, which they took for themselves to eat and sell. There were millions upon millions of oysters – so many oysters, in fact, that the locals had no real use or desire for them. Perhaps they were sick of eating oysters – who knows? But whatever, the reason, the poor came to Blue Point from miles away, and in an effort to make their living upon the waters, pulled up bushel upon bushel of succulent oysters.

The Town of Brookhaven, determined to provide some revenue for themselves, passed a law that no one should take the oysters without a license, for which the harvester had to pay a certain sum. The law was resisted at first by many people, including the Deacon himself, who claimed the oysters were put there by God and available to all. But finally the strength of the government prevailed. A group of armed men and three armed vessels were sent to patrol the waters, and they drove off the poor for good.

With the miscreants gone, the local fishermen returned to oyster harvesting to make a profit from the oyster beds; after all, if the poor could make a living on it, so could they.

Not a single oyster was found. The fishermen raked and raked, but the rakes brought up nothing but empty shells.

Ironically, the same event occurred in Southampton Bay around 1831. The Town of Southampton levied a tax on the oysters, and the oysters, which were abundant only a day before, suddenly disappeared overnight.

For years, people in both locales averred that God killed the oysters, because the government would not let the poor have them.

Woodcut of oysters from *Animals: Their Nature and Uses* by Charles Baker, 1877 (Courtesy: Sarah Hartwell)

CHAPTER III
Ships, Sails and Pirates!

Thomas Jefferson was the first American president to make public education a priority. Realizing that children who could read and write would become better decision-makers, informed voters and capable adults, Jefferson made provisions for state elementary education in Virginia in 1817. Other states soon followed suit.

In the mid-1800's on Long Island, it was not mandatory for children to go to school, but most parents wanted a basic education for their sons and daughters. Reading and writing was taught in a one-room schoolhouse. Parents paid a tuition of one dollar and fifty cents for a child to go to school for a year. If parents wanted their child to also learn arithmetic, they paid twenty-five cents more.

Schoolbooks were typically those books one's parents or older siblings possessed. Often these were family bibles or dog-eared copies of classic literature or epic poems. Nearly every young child in the 1800's, whether he could read or not, was familiar with the daring exploits of heroes such as King Arthur and his Knights of the Round Table, Ivanhoe, and Robin Hood.

However, the blood-curdling tales of pirates like the evil Blackbeard and Captain Kidd held an especially thrilling appeal for children who lived by the sea and grew up with Long Island sand in their shoes. What youngster did not dream of digging down deeply into the soil and coming up with a buried treasure? Since Captain Kidd's treasure was supposedly buried (in various locations) on Long Island, discovering his riches became the dream of generations of Long Island children. One book in particular, The Pirates' Own Book: Authentic Narratives of the Most Celebrated Sea Robbers by Charles Elms, published in 1837, was particularly popular among 19th Century readers; it was reprinted nine times before 1889!

One cannot forget about the fierce and dangerous side of living and working by the sea. Shipwrecks and pirates were a very real part of life on Long Island's south shore.

There were actually two types of pirates. The first was the kind we usually envision when we think of a pirate: a swashbuckling captain who sailed his ship in search of plunder and treasure, like Blackbeard, Henry Morgan, Black Bart and the like. But the age of seafaring pirates ended by around 1720, as the tolerance for privateering ended.

However, it was land-pirates who were often found off the Fire Island coast. These pirates were men who lived on land but tried to wreck ships by deliberately misleading them away from deep, safe waters and into dangerous, shallow or rocky shoals. Often these pirates were simply called "wreckers"; sometimes they were called "mooncussers", for they could only do the evil work on a dark, moonless night. When the moon was full, they were in danger of being seen, and they would shake their fists and "cuss" at the moon.

These wreckers, or mooncussers, would set fires on the beach and then wait. The fires were meant to do one thing – to mislead the ship's captain into thinking that he was heading his ship toward the lighthouse and safe waters. Instead, the ship was heading for disaster! Realizing the mistake too late, the captain would watch helplessly as the ship would run aground or wreck on the ragged, rocky shoals. Once the ship was wrecked, the pirates would either simply wait for the cargo of the ship to float up on the beach or - if they were in a rush - take out their small, fast boats and attack the helpless ship, murdering the crew and taking all of the booty they could find.

It did not matter which type of pirate they were to know a few things about them: they were evil and often ruthless, but also lived by a peculiar code of laws and superstitions, and had their own set of rules about what they considered fair and unfair. Pirates knew these rules. So did most every young boy who grew up in the 1700's and 1800's on Long Island!

One particular rule was that a pirate would protect and defend their treasure through life and death. It was said that pirates would bury their treasure on a deserted beach, and then draw straws to determine which man would stay behind to guard the treasure. But often this poor soul was in for a terrible and deadly surprise, as in the story "The Peculiar Tale of Hossfeeter Joe".

Whether caused by land-pirates or just the cruelty of fate, many ships have been destroyed in the treacherous shoals off Long Island. Shipwrecks and legends seem to go hand in hand, and Long Island's south shore is apparently littered with both.

"Dead Men Tell No Tales"
by Howard Pyle; *Colliers Weekly,* December 17, 1899 (PD-1923)

11
"So Lawless and Desperate a People"

In 1699, the governor of New York was actually English royalty! His name was Richard Coote, the Earl of Bellomont, and he was the Colonial Governor of New York, Massachusetts Bay and New Hampshire from 1699 to 1701.

Only fifty years into established settlements on Paumonock, and already Long Islanders had the reputation of being difficult to control! Lord Bellomont wrote to his superiors in London, calling Long Island a "great receptacle for pirates." "They are so lawless and desperate a people," he wrote, "that I can get no honest man to venture among them." He asked the British government to send him one hundred men to try to catch smugglers on Long Island's East End.

Eastern Long Island was, as Lord Bellomont intimated, "not averse to the trade" of piracy. It was indeed hard to get necessities like salt, sugar and tea, and smuggling was rife, not only on Long Island, but in all thirteen colonies. In fact, it was partially because of this culture of illegal smuggling that Parliament enacted laws that simply taxed colonists on these goods without their having a say in the usage of the tax monies. "Taxation without representation" was one of the primary reasons we eventually went to war with Great Britain during the American Revolution.

Richard Coote, First Earl of Bellomont.. This fine portrait was made by
Samuel Smith Kilburn in 1888.
(New York Public Library, Digital ID 423861)

But it was not merely because getting certain goods was difficult that smuggling and piracy became so much a part of the East End's cultural past. Geographically, it was absurd to expect a ship's captain to travel many miles out of his way to an approved Long Island customs house, if his ship was only several miles away from Connecticut. It didn't seem fair! Long Island East End settlers associated more closely with New England than New York City anyway, and goods were smuggled into secluded coves and inlets on Long Island's shores as a matter of course.

The East End was an extremely convenient place for piracy, as was Fire Island on the South Shore. Both were marked by miles of hidden coves and wild brush to obscure one's illegal activities. Tales of buried treasure in both locations soon became legendary.

We know that Captain Kidd buried treasure on Gardiner's Island in 1699, but it was retrieved and sent to Lord Bellomont when Kidd was arrested for piracy. Kidd was also said to have buried treasure at Montauk Point. In fact, a small body of water near Montauk Lighthouse has been called Money Pond for as long as anyone can remember.

There were other infamous pirates with connections to Long Island, although none were as famous as Kidd. Joseph Bradish was one such pirate. Unlike the elegant Kidd, Bradish was brash, cunning and more in line with the stereotype we think of when we imagine a pirate. His shipmates could best be described as a "scurvy crew". According to one old description, "one was pock-marked, another squint-eyed", and still another "lamish of both legs". Arrggghh!

Tales of these pirates always involve treasure being left with some innocent (or not so innocent) party to be kept safely until he returned. However, there are also several stories involving those who kept the treasure safely hidden, only to find their wealth tremendously increased once the pirate was caught and hanged.

Bradish, for example, left treasure in Sagaponack in 1699 with Colonel Henry Pierson, who was a member of the Colonial Assembly in New York. A meddling neighbor of Pierson's told the local authorities that Pierson was aiding and abetting pirates. Colonel Pierson, known for his bravery in battle, had a hard time proving that he was frightened and foolish enough to hold the bag of diamonds, rubies, pearls, sapphires, and turquoise for Bradish, but influential friends spoke on his behalf, and he went free. Bradish, however, was caught and hung.

In another instance, in 1728, Gardiner's Island was attacked by a band of eighty pirates. Looking for valuables, they cut open feather beds, scattered the Gardiners' belongings, destroyed furniture and parts of the farm and even livestock in their rage. Where was the great Gardiner wealth? The Lord of the Manor, John Gardiner, grandson of Lion Gardiner, was keenly aware of how desolate and unprotected the island was; therefore, most of their fortune was kept safely on the mainland in East Hampton. The pirates ate all of the family's food, drank everything they could lay hands on and made off with all the family silver except for one tankard. When they left, they spitefully tied the Lord of the Manor to a mulberry tree.

Captain William Kidd, Pirate (1645-1701)
18th Century portrait by Sir James Thornhill
(Courtesy: The Art Archive and Private Collection and Eileen Tweedy)

12
The Ballad of Captain Kidd

My name is William Kidd, as I sailed, as I sailed
My name is William Kidd, as I sailed
My name is William Kidd, God's laws I did
forbid
And most wickedly I did, as I sailed, as I sailed

There was once a very famous song about one of the most famous of pirates, Captain William Kidd. Today we might call "The Ballad of Captain Kidd" a sea chantey. It was sung for generations. The song was immensely popular, and it was sung everywhere, from sailing ships to pubs to street corners. It seems odd that we don't sing it any longer!

Captain William Kidd was a well-respected sea captain, known for his prosperity and elegance, and he lived in a beautiful home on Pearl Street in New York City. One day, Captain Kidd met Lord Bellomont. The colonial Governor was so impressed with the young, dashing and obviously successful captain that he wrote to King William, asking him to give Captain Kidd a royal commission as privateer to the King.

You need to know the difference between a pirate and a privateer. Many people would say that neither one was good. But a privateer had a charter from the King of England, officially allowing him to plunder ships and booty from foreign vessels in the name of the English government (with everyone getting their share of the loot, no doubt.) A pirate, on the other hand, was a "free agent", meaning that he only served himself and would attack any ship, not just foreign ones, even those of his own country. This meant that a privateer could be attacked by a pirate, even though they were both on the same side!

Once the royal commission was received, Captain Kidd took his ship, the "Adventure Galley", to the high seas. He did not fare well. Upon landing in Madagascar, 90 of his 150 crew members jumped ship. The ship itself needed such repairs that Kidd abandoned it, commandeered a French ship and sailed the seas in search of plunder for the King. And he found it – gold and silver, jewels and fine cloth.

But something happened between Lord Bellomont and Kidd while Kidd was at sea – perhaps it had something to do with the ship he had to abandon, or the crew that deserted – but whatever the reason, Lord Bellomont had a change of heart, and officially declared Kidd a pirate and an outlaw.

Why, less than two years after he lobbied for the commission for Kidd, would Bellomont accuse him of being a pirate? Did he and Captain Kidd have a secret deal between the two of them? Did Lord Bellomont not receive the enormous riches he expected to get from the great Captain Kidd?

Upon learning of this treachery, and knowing full well that the punishment for piracy was death by hanging, Kidd immediately sailed to Oyster Bay and engaged a lawyer to clear his name. Steadfastly maintaining still that his new ship was French and all of his plunder were from foreign vessels, Kidd proceeded to send a cache of jewels to Lord Bellomont's wife, presumably as an endeavor to convince her of his innocence, and to beg her to intercede to her husband on his behalf. As further insurance, he next stopped on Gardiner's Island, burying a vast treasure on the island with its owner, Jonathan Gardiner's, permission.

Finally Kidd headed up to Boston, where Lord Bellomont had been trying unsuccessfully to implement the crown's policies. Captain Kidd was promptly captured and thrown into jail. Kidd begged Lord Bellomont to listen to him, and assured him a vast treasure was safely buried on Gardiner's Island. Bellomont sent a messenger to find the treasure, and it was there, right where Kidd told him it would be. It amounted to about 20,000 British pounds — more than a million dollars today!

Jonathan Gardiner, questioned about his role in this treasure trove, gave a statement to Lord Bellomont that Kidd bequeathed him gifts of cloth and a box of gold, a bundle of quilts, 30 pounds of silver, a pound of gold dust, a sash and a pair of worsted stockings for his trouble. However, this enraged Lord Bellomont, who ordered Gardiner to send this plunder, gifts or not, to him at once. Bellomont was now less convinced than ever that this booty was *all* of the treasure captured by the spectacular Captain Kidd.

Kidd was sent back to England, and, still maintaining his innocence of piracy, was convicted and sentenced to death by hanging. On May 23, 1701, his hands were tied and he was marched onto the gallows. The noose went around his neck, and with hundreds watching the spectacle, the infamous Captain Kidd was hung...twice. (The rope broke the first time.) The notorious pirate was gibbeted (his body was put into a cage and hung) at the mouth of the harbor so that any other would-be pirates might think twice before embarking on such a life of crime. His skeleton hung there for years. (Ugh!)

There are a few legends associated with Captain Kidd. It's been said that when Jonathan Gardiner brought the gifts Kidd gave him up to Boston to return it to Lord Bellomont, a bit of booty remained behind with the Gardiners. A diamond was found, accidentally left in the seam of his traveling bag. Imagine how he must have felt to have just returned from Boston, only to be obliged to have to turn around and make the long trip all over again, just to bring Lord Bellomont a single diamond! Mrs. Gardiner told her husband in no uncertain terms that he should keep it to make up for all

"The Hanging of Captain Kidd"
from *The Pirate's Own Book: Authentic Narratives of the Most
Celebrated Sea Robbers* by Charles Elms (LC-USZ62-86665)

of the trouble he had with Kidd. The Gardiners gave it as a wedding present to their daughter Elizabeth, who married the Gardiner's Island chaplain.

And there is yet another legend regarding Captain Kidd! It was said that Kidd once visited Block Island, where his ship was restocked with supplies and he was wined and dined by Mercy (Sands) Raymond, the daughter of another successful mariner and friend of Kidd's, James Sands. After dinner Kidd, sprawled comfortably in a chair and contentedly smoking his pipe, told the woman to hold out her apron in front of her. He then reached into a large bag he had beside him, pulling out jumbles of necklaces, pearls and gold coins. Laughing, Captain Kidd threw the gold and jewels into the woman's apron until it was full and she could hold no more. After her husband Joshua Raymond died, Mercy moved with her family to northern New London, Connecticut, where she became a wealthy landowner. The Raymond family was often said to have been "enriched by the apron".

Every so often, a story comes up about a strange finding – a chest of gold found under the streets in Northport, a handful of gold coins found under a stoop somewhere else – and immediately Long Islanders wonder if there is still some of Captain Kidd's immense treasure buried somewhere around here, hidden for centuries. Many people still suspect he found treasure, and plenty of it – but just didn't want Lord Bellomont to get all of it! Maybe his great wealth is buried in not one or two, but *many* places across Long Island! And maybe it still can be found!

Since 1699, and especially after the morbidly illustrated *The Pirate's Own Book: Authentic Narratives of the Most Celebrated Sea Robbers* by Charles Elms was published in 1837, the hope of actually finding the legendary Captain Kidd's buried treasure in one's own Long Island back yard became almost an obsession.

Even to this day, many born and bred Long Islanders still dig in their yards and suggest their children to do the same (although far more Indian arrowheads have turned up than Spanish doubloons). The legend continues to be so strong that one has to wonder if it really could be *true*. Perhaps Captain Kidd was rather dishonest after all. Perhaps he was just too good at what he did. Maybe he was a spectacular privateer. Or perhaps Captain William Kidd really was... a pirate!

Take a warning now by me, for I must die, for I must die,
Take a warning now by me for I must die
Take a warning now by me and shun bad company,
Lest you come to hell with me, for I must die, I must die.

Captain Kidd Burying Treasure on Gardiner's Island
by Howard Pyle. Illustration from *Harper's New Monthly Magazine,*
1894. (PD-1923)

13
The Peculiar Tale of Hossfeeter Joe

People who lived and worked near the waters of Fire Island and its river tributaries tell the story of a man named Joe who made a living as a hossfeeter by the Carmen's River. What happened to Joe was a fascinating tale of greed and the supernatural. You see, the story goes that...

A hossfeeter? You don't know what a hossfeeter is?

Years ago many people on Long Island spoke a little differently than they do now, often slurring certain letters or dropping others with the accent they still had from where they lived before. Many people up in Boston today still famously "flatten" their "r's", saying "yahd" instead of "yard". So if you inserted an "r" into the middle of "hoss", what word would you get? Horse, of course!

What could you find on the shore or in the water that was known as horse-feet? We used to see them a lot of Long Island, although there are fewer and fewer of these today. Here's a hint: they are a shellfish, although they are more closely related to spiders and scorpions (this is getting very confusing). And they are not at all good to eat!

Were they clams? No.
Were they mussels? No.

They were crabs! And what kind of crab looks like horse-feet? A horseshoe crab! Bravo!

Men like Joe would wait for the tide to go out and gather up all the horseshoe crabs they found on the beach. They would spread them out and dry them, then grind them up and sell them to farmers for fertilizer. It was a rather dirty and very smelly job, but it brought extra money, and Joe was one of a number of men who gathered hossfeet in the brackish waters at the mouth of the Carmen's River.

If you are familiar with the poem "The Midnight Ride of Paul Revere" by Henry Wadsworth Longfellow, you might recognize the rhythm at the beginning of this poem. I borrowed Longfellow's rhyme scheme when I wrote this poem one day while at Fire Island, digging for buried treasure. Didn't find any then, don't expect to find any now – but I keep digging!

The Tale of Hossfeeter Joe
(with apologies to Henry Wadsworth Longfellow)

Listen, my children!, and you will know
Of the tragic tale of Hossfeeter Joe.
A ne'er-do-well who lived long ago
By the old Carmen's River – that's Hossfeeter Joe.

Now Joe got his name by the trade that he plied
Gathering hossfeet, which he laid out and dried
And ground up for farmers who spread it on land,
Enriching the soil for all the crops planned.

Now, the Carmen's River is right by the side
Of Fire Island, where pirates would hide
And bury their treasure long, long ago –
Or, at least, the old-timers always said so.

So Joe was brought up on the great tales of treasure
Of old Captain Kidd and his pirate-y pleasure
He firmly believed the old legends unbreaking
That treasure was buried there, ripe for the taking.

You just had to find it first!

One night Joe was sleepy. He sat down by his cart
And he started to doze – but then woke with a start.
He thought he heard something! and rubbing his
    eyes
He had the most wild, fantastic surprise!

For there in the distance, he saw very clearly
Three men dressed as pirates, all ragged and mealy
All pale as a ghost – as they certainly were
And Joe sat there, watching, and tried not to stir.

They were lugging a chest from the sea to the shore
And talking and laughing, and heaved it some more
'Til they got to the woods where they stopped their
    big rig
And took out pick-axes, and started to dig.

Joe couldn't see well, but he heard it all right –
Ghost-pirates! With treasure! So he waited a mite –
Then after a while walking back to the sea
He saw just TWO pirates. He didn't see three!

Joe knew what that meant! For the old story goes

That pirates would swear by their fingers and toes
In life or in death to protect and defend
That treasure they buried
    when they were all friends.

But friends they were not! For as one pirate found
As he went to get straws to see who'd stay around
To guard all the treasure, others came from behind
And murdered the first pirate – just to save time.

Then into the hole that they dug for their loot
They buried their treasure, and a dead pirate to
    boot.
Then they covered the hole with great shovels of
    sand
To hide all their treasure, and one murdered man.

Their treasure protected, the pirates took leave
Returning months later, their loot to retrieve.
Yo, ho! Fifteen men on a dead pirate's chest!
Even in death he guards wealth for the rest!

(Meanwhile, back on the Carmen's River...)

Well, Joe was euphoric! Joe was ecstatic!
Joe was delighted! Joe was emphatic!
He'd not work again! – for there, up for grabs
Was a whole pirate treasure! Not hossfeeter crabs!

Was he afraid of the ghost in the dark?
Oh, no, not old Joe!, and lugging his cart
He got to the edge of the river, then sneered
Strode into the forest... then Joe disappeared.

For days no one saw him, but discovered his cart

At the edge of the forest where the river did part
There were signs of a struggle and tracks in the
    sand
But no trace of Joe was there left on the land.

About a week later, some fishermen found
Joe floating up river as if he had drowned -
But the sword of a pirate in his chest had its place
With a horseshoe crab, clinging there, onto his face.

So now we know there is a treasure of gold
Buried by Carmen's River, the legend of old.
But don't try to find it! – I told you, no, no!
Or you just might end up
Like poor Hossfeeter Joe.

Dead Pirate Ashore
Illustration by Howard Pyle, *Harper's Magazine*, 1887. (PD-1923)

Gleaning From the Wreck by Thomas Moran
(Courtesy East Hampton Library, Long Island Collection)

14
"Fort Nonsense"

The Revolutionary War was a hand-to-hand ground battle for the Americans. The new and struggling nation had no navy to speak of, and what seafaring power they did possess was no match for the superior British fleet, the finest navy in the world. After the war was over, President George Washington, and John Adams and Thomas Jefferson after him, all put their efforts into developing a strong American navy. The Battle of 1812, in contrast to the Revolutionary War, became a naval battle. Ship-building became a new economy, in addition to fishing and farming, on Long Island.

One might consider that with this new-found ship-building growth, there might be extraordinary stories of the new and substantial reach of the naval military presence on Long Island. No, as usual, the Americans relied on their tenacity, pluck and ingenuity to succeed against the odds. One story that remains from the time has to do with the Long Islanders' determination to never give up, and one lone cannon mounted on a tiny fort in Poquot, dubbed for years as "Fort Nonsense".

It was simply ridiculous. The small fort established on George's Neck, equipped with one cannon capable of firing a single 32 pound ball, was meant as protection for a large area incorporating all of Setauket and Drowned Meadow (later known as Port Jefferson Harbor). It was insanity. With only two soldiers on duty as protection against the grand British fleet, they would have been better off, the local people complained, if there was nothing there at all. The tiny and seemingly useless fort became known as "Fort Nonsense".

As many feared, one night a British sloop-of-war sailed into the harbor and calmly gathered up seven American vessels. Unable to adequately retaliate, locals could only watch in dismay as the British sailors lashed the boats together and began to draw the string of vessels out of the harbor.

But suddenly, a loud "boom!" issued from Fort Nonsense. The American soldiers had loaded their single cannon, took aim, and fired. The little cannonball landed squarely on the last boat, blowing it to smithereens. The local crowd cheered with delight. If they could not have their boats, than blast it all, the British weren't going to have them either!

Fort Nonsense was nonsense no more. There seem to be no other records about the fort, or if they ever got more than one cannon. But the British got one less ship – and for the people of Drowned Meadow, that was enough.

15
The Ghost in the Rigging

The shoals off Fire Island are deceptive and treacherous. Strewn with boulders and sand bars, a ship could wreck on even a bright, beautiful spring day. But if a ship was floundering in a storm, unable to see or hear the safety of land by means of the light or horn of a lighthouse, a ship was completely at the mercy of the Almighty.

The *Louis V. Place* was a three-masted schooner heading from Baltimore to New York Harbor in January of 1895, with one hundred and ten tons of coal in its hold. The ship was piloted by Captain William H. Squires, an affable man with a pleasant appearance. His moustache and muttonchops were neatly shaven, and he possessed a high forehead, giving him a look of genial intelligence. He was an experienced captain, not given to unwarranted fears.

All along the eastern seaboard, foul weather and record-breaking frigid temperatures were reported. New York City was at zero degrees, Florida had the coldest date on record, and it was snowing from Canada down to North Carolina. The fledgling U.S. Life Saving Service (the predecessor of the U.S. Coast Guard) had their hands full, with nearly twenty nine vessels and one-hundred and thirty men utilized to full capacity attending to storm and sea disasters up and down along the U.S. coast. Along the southern coast of Long Island, more than 30 ships wrecked that day.

The *Louis V. Place* had left Baltimore on January 28, but the storm-tossed seas pushed her further south and east of her anticipated route. Her hull, rigging and sails were full of ice, and her crew toiled day and night for four days to coax the ship in dangerous cross seas. On February 8, the winds changed ferociously, enraging the seas and making it impossible to navigate. Exhausted men with frostbitten hands tried desperately to control their sails. The furious waves along with the blinding snow and the howling wind turned the already-frozen ship into a floating iceberg, her running gear frozen in the blocks. The crew's efforts were fruitless.

Never in his life had Captain Squires felt incapable of handling anything the ocean could dish out, but this storm terrified him. He felt certain he was near land, although he thought he was at Sandy Hook in New Jersey.

Just then they heard breakers and the ship pitched violently. They were at Long Island, off Fire Island, stranded on a sandbar with the waves breaking over her deck. The crew scrambled for the rigging.

The call came on shore that a large merchant vessel was floundering in the water off Fire Island. Rescuers from the nearest USLSS from Lone Hill Station (today this is the area near

Oakdale) were already aiding another wreck, the *John B. Manning*, which had stranded several hours before, about a mile further east from where the *Louis V. Place* was heaving back and forth, her crew stranded and frozen in the rigging above.

It took nearly twelve hours for the life savers to complete their first rescue; not knowing they had another wreck on their hands, they left most of their frozen equipment at the scene of the first wreck and trudged back to the station in blinding snow, with temperatures on the beach around zero with wind chills of at least ten below.

Photograph of the wreck of the Louis V. Place by Martin Anderson
(Photo courtesy of the Long Island Maritime Museum)

Imagine how they must have felt when they realized there was another wreck that needed their help! Despite frantic effort upon effort, using every kind of equipment they could attempt, rescuers were unable to reach the *Louis V. Place*. They struggled for hours in heavy seas, but the bitter cold and wind was too treacherous. They shot the Lyle gun five times, sending out a line to reach the ship if only the crew would grab it, but the crew was physically unable to move toward the lines. The desperation was almost too much to bear. By the next day, people gathered on the shore in the bitter cold to witness the horror. One eyewitness claimed one could see eight figures up in the riggings. A photographer, Martin Anderson, arrived and took pictures of the disaster. The tragedy became a scene of morbid curiosity as local residents came to observe the wrecked ship. Men came to help futilely with ropes and garden tools. Children watched, not understanding the entire scene in front of them. People were shouting. Women wept.

Rescuers tried unsuccessfully to reach the *Louis V Place* for two whole days.

Finally, on the afternoon of the second day the wind and seas began to abate, and the rescuers feverishly sent out a lifeboat. The scene that met their eyes when they reached the ship defied all comprehension.

Most of the crew was dead, their bodies washed off the riggings; two were lost to the sea, two others were frozen solidly to the deck. One deckhand was in the crosstrees near the other two, frozen to death. The body of another was found hanging in the rigging, upside down, swaying morbidly in the wind, still held in place by the lashings he had knotted around himself.

It was a horrific sight, made worse by the knowledge that the rescuers could see them the entire time, but simply could not reach them.

The dead were buried in a graveyard in Patchogue.

But – here is the most bizarre part of the story:

Just at the height of the storm, on-lookers on the shore claimed to have seen a likeness of a man in the spray in the front of the rigging. Hearing them, the photographer, Martin Anderson, refocused his camera and took a few pictures. When he developed his film, he was astounded to see, at the front of the rigging, the likeness of a man – with a moustache and muttonchops, cleanly shaven, and with a high forehead. (See illustrations, next page).

Some people claimed the photograph was a hoax. But others swore that it was the death portrait of Captain William Squires.

The Ghost in the Rigging
(Both photos, courtesy Long Island Maritime Museum)

CHAPTER IV
Tales of the American Revolution

Some of the strangest and most poignant stories that have come down to us through the centuries have to do with the British occupation of Long Island during the American Revolution.

Long Island was rife with bad feelings, neighbor against neighbor. Some people were Loyalist Tories, siding with the British and hoping for reconciliation with the Crown; many others – Patriots – sided with the thirteen Colonies' fight for freedom. But whether you were a Tory or a Patriot was almost immaterial when it came to the British. It has been said that one of the ironies of the American Revolution was that no matter what side you were on, the British still took your farm, your crops and your belongings in the name of the King. Everyone suffered.

Here on Long Island, especially across the North Shore, British occupation was substantial, with large settlements in key locations like Oyster Bay, Huntington and Setauket. In at least one instance, a British major actually lived in a house that played a part in George Washington's spy ring!

Did the presence of British soldiers on the streets of these towns stop the patriots from trying to band together and gain their freedom? Absolutely not. In fact, as it did in Boston just a few years earlier, the British presence inflamed passions and only served to encourage residents to find small, personal ways to thwart the British and help the American cause. The very real stories of the bravery and daring of these Long Island men and women are indeed "the stuff of legend".

As for the story of the frozen ducks... well, it was definitely the sort of tale that one needed to have a little fun during those cold and oppressive winter nights. Be on the lookout for a few ghosts in the stories as well!

16
The Patriot with the Petticoat

Anna Smith Strong - known to most people as Nancy - was a true American patriot. She was just as brave and daring as the men she worked with during the American Revolution.

Nancy's husband Selah had been arrested by the British and was being held in a prison ship in New York Harbor. Nancy was determined to do whatever she could to ensure the hated British would leave Long Island and that her husband would come home safely.

But what could she do? She was a woman alone with a family to care for, in a day and age when most women kept their place quietly at home. And yet Nancy performed a valuable service for none other than General George Washington, who was quartered in New Jersey, safely away from the threat of the British fleet in New York Harbor. How could Nancy help George Washington when he was some fifty miles away? Well, it was simple.

Nancy was a spy.

In 1778, General George Washington had severe doubts about whether he could indeed win the war against the British. King George sent his navy to "keep the peace", so some eighty-eight frigates settled in New York Harbor, just sitting and waiting for a bad move on the part of General Washington.

*The Passage of British Troops from Staten Island to Gravesend Bay,
22 August 1776.*
19th Century wood engraving. (PD-1923)

In August of 1776, shortly after the
Declaration of Independence was sent to King
George and war was declared, the British fought
a bloody battle on Long Island soil. The fight
came to be known as the Battle of Brooklyn, or
the Battle of Long Island. (Brooklyn, like
Queens, was considered a part of Long Island in
those days). The troops from Long Island,
gathered from as far away as Stony Brook,

fought bravely but were no match for the well-trained British troops. Some 5,000 troops came to fight from Long Island, and only about 500 came back alive. The British easily won the battle, and promptly quartered in the harbor villages, such as Oyster Bay, Huntington and Stony Brook, commandeering the best farms and houses "in the name of the King". So, with the frigates in the Sound and the British on our doorsteps, General George Washington told the residents of Long Island to flee. Long Island was lost, he said.

But there still existed brave men and women, who were not so willing to give up their farms and livelihood without a fight. They were willing to risk life and limb in order to achieve freedom from Great Britain.

General Washington knew he needed information about the British on Long Island, for it was a strategic location and many other areas – New England, Boston, New Jersey – could be affected from troop movements out of Long Island Sound. And so – very quietly – General Washington began to put together an ingenious spy ring that passed secret information across Long Island, across the Sound, over Connecticut, to the Bronx and finally reaching Washington's headquarters in New Jersey.

This was a very dangerous job. The spy ring relied on the bravery, silence and wit of a handful of loyal Patriots. It often took weeks to get information to General Washington, but it was information he sorely needed – information that aided the Revolution, and was therefore considered treasonous to the British crown. If the British soldiers caught someone spying, he or she could be tried for treason on the spot and hanged from the nearest tree. And many people were.

It was a dark and frightening time.

There was a young man who worked for a British newspaper in New York City. His name was Robert Townsend. As a newspaperman, he was privy to lots of information about the British. When he was not in his office writing for the newspaper, he was speaking to British soldiers and others, and much information went his way. However, Robert was not what he seemed.

He, like Nancy, was a spy for General George Washington.

Townsend (known in the spy ring by the code name "Culper, Junior") might learn information that he thought was important enough to pass along to General Washington. Or perhaps, a letter might come to Townsend from Washington himself, requiring a response. Townsend could not send it back the way it came – it was just too dangerous. So a fascinating chain of events began:

Robert Townsend ("Culper, Junior") would wait until he saw Austin Roe, a Setauket tavern owner who rode the 30 miles each way into

Portrait of an unidentified woman from the 1780s
(Photo courtesy New York Public Library digital ID: 421392)

Manhattan twice a week, supposedly to pick up supplies. Townsend would write the message in a cipher, or code, before passing it along the spy route; sometimes the message was written in a special way that required the use of another letter, with words cut out, in order to understand the message; sometimes the message was even written in invisible ink! "Culper, Junior" would then give the message to Roe, who took the message and rode all the way back to Setauket, depositing the letter in a small box located on the edge of the property of Abraham Woodhull (who was known as "Culper, Senior", even though he was actually younger than Townsend). Once Woodhull got the message, he kept it in the safe spot, but now maintained a watchful eye on — of all things — his neighbor Nancy's clothesline.

Nobody is really sure how Nancy Smith Strong knew when the next part of the spy ring · a whale man by the name of Caleb Brewster · arrived in Setauket from Connecticut. Some folks think that Nancy's young son may have gone out daily in his little boat and looked out for Brewster among the Setauket coves. A child moving about in a little skiff would be all but unnoticed by the British soldiers, who wouldn't consider a child in a rowboat a threat or a traitor. But however she knew Caleb Brewster was in a Setauket cove, as soon as she knew it, Nancy ran into her kitchen and promptly wet a black petticoat (more like a skirt we might wear today) and any number of six handkerchiefs. Running her wet clothes to her clothesline, she hung up the black petticoat and sometimes two, sometimes five handkerchiefs. It was a code! – a signal to Abraham Woodhull that Caleb Brewster was in town, and hiding in one of six coded coves in Setauket. Each cove was designated by a particular number of handkerchiefs. Woodhull would then silently grab the message in the box on his property, and secretly bring it to the cove where Caleb Brewster was waiting.

Cutting across Long Island Sound in a small whaleboat, wheedling his way through the British barricade, Brewster had the most dangerous link in the spy chain. Caleb Brewster consistently evaded British scouts and other terrors as he rowed across the Sound. He landed somewhere near Bridgeport, Connecticut, where there was not so much British activity. Brewster would meet up with Washington's dragoons – special soldiers - who would ride the message to George Washington's right-hand-man, Colonel Benjamin Tallmadge, who was located in Fairfield, Connecticut. Tallmadge would then bring the message inland and out of harm's way to Washington himself.

There were many, many people who risked their lives to send information to General Washington and helped win the war with the British. We do not know all of them. Spies were referred to in these letters by numbers only, not names. It was very serious and secretive. Anyone involved in this spy ring was a true patriot. Had they been caught, they would have been convicted of treason and hanged.

But Nancy Smith Strong has the sole and distinct honor of being the one woman in the spy ring whose name we know. She is often referred to as "The Patriot with the Petticoat." So - three cheers for Nancy Smith Strong! Huzzah, huzzah, huzzah!

17
"Tombstone Bread"

From 1776 to 1783, the town of Huntington was occupied by British troops. The people of Huntington, like those in Setauket and Smithtown, were already quite well known as "rebel trouble-makers," outspoken against the King and the inequity of British law. In 1782, nearly at the end of the Revolutionary War, the people of Huntington received yet another new commander of the British troops who were quartered in their town – and this one was, by far, the worst of the lot.

Twenty-nine year old Colonel Benjamin Thompson was an American-born British commander of the King's American Dragoons. The aggressively ambitious Thompson was determined to make a name for himself, and earn for himself all of the titles and respect a successful British officer would have. The way to do this, Thompson figured, was to succeed where others had failed. To impress his British superiors, Thompson vowed that he was going to break the spirit of those rebellious people of Huntington, for once and for all.

Oh, those Huntingtonians! Those rebels! Those traitors! They had town meetings! They met on the village green, in taverns, on street corners! They were dangerous! If there was a group that needed to be watched carefully, it

Sir Benjamin Thompson, later Count Rumford (1753–1814)
Painting by Thomas Gainsborough, 1783 (Harvard Art Museums/Fogg
Museum, Bequest of Edmund C. Converse - HUAM231679)

was the people of Huntington.

Colonel Thompson wanted desperately to put an end to those traitorous rebels. Having a scientific and calculating mind, he methodically considered his strategy. Slowly, his mind hatched a terrible plan.

He decided to construct a fort, and the best location for a fort in Huntington was on the top of a hill, currently occupied by the First Presbyterian Church and burial ground. Thompson knew that religious freedom was one of the issues over which the battle lines between America and Great Britain were drawn. What would be more demoralizing to the townspeople of Huntington than destroying their church?

Tipping the decision was the still resounding presence of one particularly outspoken individual - Reverend Ebenezer Prime, the former head of the First Presbyterian Church in Huntington. Reverend Prime died in 1779, but the influence of the sermons he preached against the tyranny of Great Britain was still keenly felt among the citizens of the beleaguered town. A particularly large grave marker, on the crest of the hill of the old burial ground next to the church, continued to reaffirm his presence, if not his esteemed rank in life.

Colonel Thompson immediately marched his troops into the burial ground and ordered them to set up camp. Imagine setting up your tents in a graveyard! From letters sent from some these soldiers back to their families in England, the location was not pleasant, neither for the Huntington residents or the soldiers themselves.

To the horror of the residents, Colonel Thompson ordered the beautiful white church with its tall steeple dismantled, and used the timbers to construct a fort at the very peak of the burial ground, the highest point in the village. As if the desecration of the church and burial ground wasn't enough, Thompson forced the Huntington residents to provide the labor. Local carpenters were put to work tearing down the church and sides of other buildings in the area. Still other residents were ordered to bring axes and spades to destroy the burial ground and prepare the earth for new construction. Adding insult to injury, the local militia was forced to deliver these orders to the population. Thompson probably sat in his quarters and laughed maniacally. He was going to bring these rebels to their knees! Over one hundred grave stones were removed and the burial ground leveled in preparation for the fort's construction. As a testament to his vicious and inappropriate wit, Thompson dubbed the fort "Fort Golgotha", after the hill where Jesus Christ was crucified.

Thompson had a particularly evil and special plan for the large grave marker of Ebenezer Prime. He ordered the marker laid sideways in the ground at the front portal of the fort, so that, Thompson said, he could "trod on the Old

Rebel" any time he entered or left the fort.

The grave stones that were removed were not destroyed, but recycled in a particularly ghastly way. The stones were desecrated, utilized in the construction of fireplaces, ovens and floors within the fort. It was said that the women of the town were required by law to bring their bread to be cooked in the fort's ovens. Tales are told of loaves of bread being turned out of the ovens with the reverse inscription of the tombstones embossed on the bottom crust. Imagine turning your bread over and reading the name of your neighbor or relative! The bread became known as "Tombstone Bread". Local superstition claims that to this day, women's screams and cries can be heard on the wind in the graveyard, the tormented spirits of those reliving the horror of discovering the name of their loved ones on the bottom of their bread.

There is a happy ending to this ghastly tale. In March 1783, just four months after disassembly of the Old First Church and construction of Fort Golgotha, British troops were ordered to evacuate Huntington. The war was nearly over! But Thompson was not going to leave Huntington without one more dramatic act of defiance. As his last act to aggravate Huntington's townspeople, Col. Thompson set blazing fires to all the wood in the area so that the inhabitants would have little or nothing to heat their homes during the remaining months

The Comforts of a Rumford Stove

Cartoon by James Gillray (1756-1815). Count Rumford (Benjamin Thompson), inventor of the Rumford stove, stands with his back to the fire, his coat-tails spread to permit enjoyment from the warmth.
(Courtesy Library of Congress: LC-USZC4-6322)

of winter.

Thompson returned to England after the war. Oddly enough, he earned the praise and honors he was seeking, not through his aggressive military command but by his scientific mind. While he was working with the British armies in America, Thompson conducted experiments concerning the force of gunpowder, and his research was published in England, in 1781, in the *Philosophical Transactions* of the Royal Society. The research earned him the respect of the scientific community. Therefore, when he moved back to London at the conclusion of the war, he already had a reputation as a scientist, and earned far more respect as a physicist than as a military leader. He was knighted in 1784.

The British reign of terror under "The Scourge of Huntington" was finally over. The hated Fort Golgotha was torn down and the old First Presbyterian Church was reconstructed across the street on the site where it still stands today. The gravestones were replaced as well as possible, and to this day the Old Burial Ground, with its large shade trees quietly guarding it from the busy street, still stands as a charming and peaceful testament to the courageous men and women of Huntington during the American Revolution. And yes, Reverend Prime's enormous gravestone is still there.

Hessian Officer
(Early print, probably German; source unknown. PD-1923)

18
Nothing Says "Christmas" Like... a Hessian?

The west and eastern ends of Long Island, in the 17th and 18th Centuries, were as different as if they were two separate countries. The western part of the Island was dominated by Manhattan, and there were a great many Dutch settlers. There was also a large Quaker component in New York and Queens, and these Quakers, tolerant of peoples' individual differences and eager to trade, were just the type of people to make a large city succeed. However, on the east end of Long Island, settlers were descendants of the Pilgrims. Stern, morally strict and unwilling to break from tradition, these early settlers felt that celebrations were better suited in church and not in the streets.

Christmas was a particular bone of contention. A good number of English kings – especially King Henry VIII – allowed Christmas celebrations to turn into a bacchanal, celebrating "Yuletide" with pagan festivities that had absolutely nothing to do with Christ's birth. The debauchery in the streets was more reminiscent of Mardi Gras than Christmas! So when the Puritans came to America, to save themselves the trouble of policing the day, they simply made celebrating Christmas illegal. The

Pilgrims might have their Thanksgiving gatherings, but Christmas was out of the question.

And so, as the East End became settled with Puritans, Christmas was just another day.

Supposedly, it wasn't until the Revolutionary War that Long Islanders saw a Christmas tree. It occurred in an area known as Cedar Swamp (today Old Brookville). German Hessian soldiers, hired by the British to help them fight the Revolution, were quartered in the woods of Cedar Swamp, a lovely forested area made up predominantly of evergreen cedar pines. As Christmas approached, the British were unfazed, but the German soldiers were unwilling to give up their holiday celebrations, especially since they were so far from home. It was an odd spectacle, so the locals reported, to see their enemies taking candles, apples, uniform buttons and bits of shiny this and that, and decorating a large tree by their encampment. A number of people commented on how very pretty the sight was... despite the war.

Christmas traditions, such as decorating Christmas trees, placing a crèche under the tree and leaving stockings for Saint Nicholas to fill were largely German, and the English settlers on the east end of Long Island wanted nothing to do with them. The Dutch on the western end of Long Island celebrated with a number of the charming German traditions, but their own celebrations traditionally were quiet and small. Christmas traditions did not catch on in a big way on Long Island until nearly the mid-1800's, when William Cullen Bryant and his wife Mary, the harbingers of Long Island style, held a party in their lovely home Cedermere and featured a glowing Christmas tree. The party, and the beautifully decorated tree, was so spectacular that it earned praises in newspaper articles published in *The Brooklyn Eagle* and *The New York Times*.

But the Bryant's were only copying the Christmas "fad" that was currently sweeping Great Britain. Across the sea, Queen Victoria adopted many of the lovely Lutheran traditions of her beloved German husband Prince Albert's homeland – a Christmas tree being one of them. Her subjects went wild. If their adored Queen had a Christmas tree, then, by Jove!, it was good enough for everyone else! England adopted the German traditions with a vengeance bordering on obsession, and it didn't take long for the fashionable folk in America to do the same. By the late 1800's, Christmas celebrations on Long Island involved a joyfully excessive mix of traditions from Germany, England and New York City - Christmas trees decorated with candles and star-shaped butter cookies, glistening presents, Christmas stockings left empty for Santa to fill, special baked goodies like German stollen and English fruitcake, a crèche depicting the Christ Child under the tree, angels, stars and the singing of Christmas carols, even the rotund and bearded personage of Santa Claus himself – and were easily recognizable as the same holiday traditions Long Island families enjoy today.

THE CHRISTMAS TREE.

Illustration from *Godey's Lady's Book*, December, 1850 (PD-US)

19
Frozen Ducks in the Kitchen!

It was winter of 1779-1780, the coldest winter Long Islanders had ever seen. The winter was so cold, and ice formed in layers so thick and large, that it was said people could walk from Huntington, Long Island to Stamford, Connecticut, right across Long Island Sound!

It was the middle of the American Revolution, and the British, victors of the Battle of Long Island (also known as the Battle of Brooklyn) began occupying Long Island homes and farms for use as housing and supplies for themselves. Wherever there was a fine farm or some stores of food, it was confiscated or claimed in the name of the King. It did not matter if you were a patriot or a loyalist Tory – you were freezing and starving that frigid winter, while the British troops drank from your well, ate your provisions and slept in your house.

The story goes that a man and his wife lived in a place just south of Huntington we know today as Melville, an area rather well known for having a great number of small ponds and fresh springs. With the British at their doorstep, the couple needed to seek out additional food for their own use. Peering up at the sky outside, the husband realized that yet another snowstorm was imminent, and it was growing late in the day; so he kissed his wife, took his

Hunter in the Snow by Thomas Bewick (1753-1828).
Woodcut, c.1804 (PD-1923)

musket and made his way out into the woods to look for some berries or, by some miracle, a rabbit or grouse.

As he walked, he came upon a frozen pond. In his younger days, he might have skated on such a pond. He scanned the icy surface with a brief smile, and thought wistfully about past, better days. There was, however, something that looked rather odd along the banks of the frozen water, and rubbing his eyes against the twilight, he peered more closely at the pond. The peculiar shape around the water was actually a flock of ducks! He raised his musket and, hoping desperately to bring down one duck before the others flew away, he took careful aim and fired. One duck immediately fell over. He was astounded, however, to see that the other ducks did not move! He walked up to the edge of the pond, and the ducks still did not move. The man stared in amazement. The ducks were frozen solid!

With a prayer of gratitude, the man immediately gathered up the ducks, putting them into a large sack he had brought with him. He then trudged home, the sack nearly too heavy to hold. He dragged it behind him through the fields, leaving long tracks in the snow.

Pintail Duck
by Thomas Bewick (1753-1828)
Woodcut, c. 1804 (PD-1923)

The man soon arrived back home. Huffing and puffing, he pulled the bag into the kitchen as his wife stared in astonishment. The man was quite nearly exhausted from the cold and from lugging the heavy bag over the hills and fields. With great effort he hoisted the sack full of frozen ducks to the table, where they landed with a resounding thud, and began to tell his wife the remarkable story. In disbelief, she took the ducks out of his sack one by one. They were so frozen, she could not even get her sharpest kitchen knife into the neck to butcher the bird and prepare and salt the meat. She tried a hatchet – and the head of the hatchet broke! Those ducks were frozen as solid as a rock!

With that, the wife told her husband that perhaps they should just leave the ducks out on the wooden kitchen table overnight. If they defrosted just a bit in the warm kitchen, she said, the ducks would be easier to butcher and clean tomorrow. With that, the couple spread the frozen ducks on the table, ate a small dinner of soup and bread, and after checking the waning fire, they went together to bed.

The next morning they awoke to a frenzied commotion in the kitchen. They ran into the kitchen, and what do you think they saw? Ducks! Ducks, flying all over the kitchen! Duck feathers in the leftover soup! Duck feathers on the floor! Apparently they were frozen – but they weren't dead! The warm kitchen was all they needed to revive – and fly!

The husband and wife were so astounded that they opened the kitchen door and every single duck flew out.

And that was the end of the frozen ducks in the kitchen.

20
Uh...When Did You Say You Were Leaving?

The American Revolution was fought from 1776 to 1783, with Huntington, on Long Island's north central shore, having the dubious honor of being the place occupied longest by the British. Although the war was over officially on September 3, 1783, a good number of British soldiers and Tory sympathizers who wished to either go back to England or head up to Nova Scotia needed to remain in Huntington Harbor, as the ships that were supposed to take them were delayed in arrival. The last British finally left the shores of Huntington, New York on November 25, 1783, more than two months after the war was over.

Chapter V
The Spookiest Tales

"From ghoulies and ghosties
And long-leggedy beasties
And things that go bump in the night,
Good Lord, deliver us!"
- *Scottish Prayer*

Our earliest forefathers were well acquainted with tales of devils, ghosts and witches. With strange new lands come strange tales, things one doesn't understand or that defy explanation. The stern and unyielding Pilgrims were very familiar with the temptations of the devil, so much so that punishment for the practice of witchcraft was actually built into their laws. It was far easier to lay blame on the supernatural than it was to try to understand the unthinkable, and many an innocent person was accused of "trucking with the devil." If one was found guilty, the punishment was death.

A test for a witch might have involved tying heavy rocks to a person and throwing them into the water. If they floated, they were a witch. If they drowned, they were innocent. As one could *imagine, this kind of test, done too frequently within a society, would result in the end of the society – there would be no one left!*

Unfortunately, the laws were also left open to interpretation and there are records of a number of innocent people in the new English settlements in Virginia, Massachusetts, Connecticut and Long Island, who were falsely accused of being a witch. The arbitrary nature of the accusations reflected the fear, suspicion, jealousy and paranoia of the uncertain and frightening times. Actively seeking out individuals for the purpose of destroying their character to this day is referred to as "a witch-hunt."

It is a dubious honor that the first witch trial in America may have occurred right here in East Hampton in 1657, some thirty years before Salem, Massachusetts was famously branded with its own tragic witch hysteria, trials and deaths. The following story, "Witch!" describes the very true events of this first witch trial. However, like anyplace else with a long colonial history, Long Island also has its share of supernatural and ghostly tales – many of which persist until this day.

21
Witch!

In the 1600's, as it is today, children were, and are, expected to respect their elders. However, until the Duke's Laws were enacted in 1665, if a child was disrespectful, his crime could actually be punishable by *death*. It probably did not happen often (or even at all), but the law was actually on the books.... right up there with the worst crimes: stealing a pig, and witchcraft.

The gossiping whispers in the sleepy little town of East Hampton flew thick and fast, in hushed but frantic tones among the neighbors. Many wondered if a young girl of the village had been punished for the words of disrespect she spoke to her elders a few months before. She certainly said as much before she died! She said it! Goody Simons heard it! Many other people in the town heard whispers that the girl's death was punishment not from the stern laws of their government or even by God, but from a *witch*. A witch, who lived right there among them!

A witch, whose name was Goody Garlick.

The young girl was Elizabeth Gardiner Howell, the daughter of Lion Gardiner and his wife Mary. She was born September 14, 1641 on the Isle of Wight, a large island Gardiner had named for his ancestral home; we know it today as Gardiner's Island. Although she had an older brother and sister, they had both been born in Connecticut; Elizabeth Gardiner was the first white child born in the new English settlement on Long Island.

She was married quite young; she, and her husband of less than a year, Arthur Howell, lived and worked on her father's vast estate, along with the members of the small community, consisting of thirty-three families.

Perhaps, as the daughter of the community's leader, the fifteen-year-old Elizabeth, now expecting her first child, believed she was entitled to some preferential treatment when she brought lunch to her husband, working on the Gardiner estate, during the harvest season. It is unknown what happened, but she apparently had words with Joshua Garlick, the overseer of Gardiner's vast farm; upon hearing the altercation, Joshua's wife Elizabeth, in short order, also became involved. Although the words of the argument were soon over, the bad feelings persisted. Winter was coming on hard, and soon the village uncomfortably settled down from the social activity of the harvest into the winter's bitter cold.

During those freezing months people huddled indoors; and as happened in the other Puritan settlements in New England, "contagion" (most likely smallpox) struck the small community. There was not a family out of the thirty-three that did not have someone affected by disease.

It was February of 1657 when Elizabeth

Gardiner Howell went into labor. It was a difficult birth, and while the baby survived the ordeal, things had not gone well for the young mother. Her nurse, an older woman from the village named Goody Simons, desperately applied wet cloths to her forehead, trying to cool the girl's raging fever. Suddenly, Elizabeth shot upright and flailed wildly at an unseen specter at the end of the bed.

"A witch! A witch!" she shrieked. "Now you come to torture me because I spoke two or three words against you!"

Birth and death were often entwined in this unforgiving new country, but this was so much worse than anything in the nurse's experience. Had the girl contracted the illness that was running rampant in the village? Or could it actually be, as the raving girl claimed, the work of a *witch*? Terrified, the woman ran to fetch Lion Gardiner, who himself was desperately attending his own sick wife.

He glared at Goody Simons as she unceremoniously barged into Gardiner's home. "Come quickly, sir!" she cried. "Your daughter is possessed!"

Upon hearing the story and fearing for her daughter's life, Gardiner's wife weakly insisted he go. Gardiner and the nurse raced back through the darkness to Arthur Howell's farm, where the new father sat, frightened and confused, vacantly holding his new baby as she slept peacefully in his arms. He looked helplessly at his father-in-law. Lion Gardiner strode into his daughter's bedroom.

"Child", he demanded, trying to reach her through her incoherent moans. "What did you see?"

The girl sobbed. "I saw Goody Garlick! – at the edge of the bed! – and a black thing, thither!"

That was Friday evening. The next morning, in terror of losing her daughter to this unseen force, Lion Gardiner's wife roused herself from her own sickbed and went to visit her child. Upon entering the room, Elizabeth held out her arms to her mother and burst into tears. "Oh, Mother! Mother! – I am possessed!" she sobbed.

By Sunday, Elizabeth Gardiner Howell was dead.

The girl's death was the final straw in the whispered accusations against Elizabeth Garlick, a respectable woman of the small village. For many, now it was certain: Goody Garlick was a witch. Everyone said they heard it was so. But all had heard this terrible whisper from one person in particular, someone who perhaps knew her the best of anyone in the village – Elizabeth Garlick's neighbor, Goody Davis.

The appellation "Goody" had nothing whatsoever to do with goodness. "Goody" was short for "Goodwife" – a form of address used to denote a woman of a respectable social standing in the community. A servant would not be addressed in this way.   Most women were addressed as Goodwife, or Goody, while most men were called Goodman. It was, more or less, the way we would address someone as "Mister" or "Misses" today.

Gardiner Mansion
Sketch by Alfred Waud, 1875
(Courtesy East Hampton Library. Long Island Collection)

Elizabeth and Joshua Garlick lived and worked on Lion Gardiner's vast estate. So did Arthur and Elizabeth Howell, and Goody Davis and her husband Foulk, and most of the other families in the small community   The Garlicks had a productive farm and healthy livestock, and their good management allowed them a measure of success that seemed to always elude

Goody Davis. Nothing is known of Goody Davis' husband Foulk, but it can be assumed he was either ill or a ne'er-do-well, for Goody Davis seemed to reap misfortune upon misfortune that could be almost certainly attributed to a husband not pulling his weight. It therefore seemed almost logical, in that small, sheltered and paranoid community, that any misfortune that befell Goody Davis would be attributed by her to supernatural means. No one living in a group, especially not one that observed everyone's personal life in minute detail, would want the shame or stigma of weakness, whether from physical ailment or drunkenness or, worst of all, laziness. No, there had to be a more logical reason sorrow upon sorrow was heaped upon Goody Davis' shoulders. And that reason simply had to be that her nemesis, Goody Garlick, was a witch.

In the Puritan, Calvinist world, people were painfully aware of the presence of the Devil in their everyday lives. There was no room for sin if one was going to make a community work, and therefore, sin — of any kind - became punishable by law. These were people who believed in the presence of Satan as readily as they did the presence of the magistrate. There was no separation of church and state. Crimes like stealing and murder actually had fines similar to those levied on people who gossiped or missed church services. If one was too outrageous, one did not fit into the community, and a number of people were actually banished from these early settlements across New England simply for being too unconventional.

Lion Gardiner, however, believed in hard work as the means to success, and Joshua and Elizabeth Garlick were two of his best workers. In fact, Joshua Garlick was the overseer of Lion Gardiner's estate. So when the people of his village came to him a few days after his daughter's death, proclaiming Goody Garlick as the one responsible, not only for his daughter's death, but also for the misfortunes that happened in the village in the past, he had a difficult decision to make. Should he dismiss the Garlicks? - and if he did, on what grounds? He would not bend to pressure and silly talk. But this gossip was getting dangerous. If he did nothing, the entire community would be up in arms; dissidence could destroy the entire settlement.

So Lion Gardiner, being the smartest man in the community, did what all intelligent men would do in the same situation – he passed the buck. He sent the complaint to the legal body, which consisted of three justices - John Mulford, John Hand and Thomas Baker.

Over the next three weeks, the magistrates gathered testimony from thirteen people. However, it soon became obvious that there was really only one person who perpetuated the story about Goody Garlick being a witch, and did so repeatedly with anyone who would listen to her · and that was none other than her neighbor, Goody Davis.

Thomas Talmadge testified that he heard Goody Davis complain about Goody Garlick causing her child's death, as well as causing her ox to break its leg. Another neighbor testified that she heard Goody Davis say that Goody Garlick was responsible for the death of her sow and five piglets. And Goodwife Simons testified that, the night before she died, Elizabeth Gardiner Howell told her she saw Goody Garlick at her bed, "ready to pull me in pieces... and she pricked me with needles!"

As Joshua Garlick prepared a counter·suit, accusing Goody Davis of slander, more damning testimony came from Goody Davis. As if to punctuate her accusations with the worst of all, she blamed Goody Garlick in the death of her own child.

Goody Birdsall testified that she heard Goody Davis complain of how her child came to die. She explained that Davis told her that she had just dressed the baby in white linen. "Goody Garlick came in and said how pretty the child doth look. And so soon as she had spoken Goody Garlick said the child is not well for it groaneth and Goody Davis said her heart did rise and Goody Davis said when she took the child from Goody Garlick she said she saw death in the face of it. And her child sickened presently upon it and lay five days and five nights and never opened the eyes nor cried till it died."

For the most part, Lion Gardiner stayed out of the accusations and testimony. However, when asked if he thought Goody Garlick was a witch, Lion Gardiner angrily replied that Goody Davis had taken in an Indian child to nurse, and "for the lucre of little wampum, Goody Davis actually starved her own child to death".

The magistrates listened seriously to all of this outrageous testimony. They were, of course, the smartest men in the entire county. So what do you think they did upon concluding their hearing? They passed the buck. They sent the case up to the seat of the colonial government, in Hartford, Connecticut.

Imagine what that must have been like for Goody Garlick, dressed in her Puritan black and shaking with fear, ferrying up to Hartford for her witchcraft trial. Witchcraft was one of the most heinous crimes one could be accused of, and the most horrifically punished. Death could be from hanging, burning or being pressed to death with heavy stones. Just imagine how Goody Garlick must have suffered! Her husband stayed stoically by her side. The townspeople cast furtive glances at her. They were all there to testify what they heard against her from Goody Davis. In fact, nearly everyone was there *except* Goody Davis. There appears to be no explanation why she did not go to Hartford to testify in person.

The Hartford trial was held on May 5, in the Particular Court of Connecticut, with a panel of magistrates headed by the governor, John Winthrop. The bailiffs brought the group into the court. Goody Garlick stood alone and shuddering in the middle of the floor as the witnesses filled the benches against the walls.

The Witch No. 1
Lithograph by Joseph A. Baker, 1892
(Courtesy Library of Congress, LC-DIG-ppmsca-09402)

The chief justice, John Winthrop, rose and read the following indictment:

"Thou art indicted by the name of Elizabeth Garlick the wife of Joshua Garlick of East Hampton, that not having the fear of God before thine eyes thou has entertained familiarity with Satan the great enemy of God and mankind and by his help since the year 1650 hath done works above the course of nature to the loss of lives of several persons ...and in particular the wife of Arthur Howell of East Hampton, for which both according to the laws of God and the established law of this commonwealth thou deservest to die."

Testimony was heard and the case was quite serious. But finally, with all of the evidence being nothing more than vicious slander of one woman against another, (and perhaps because Goody Davis was not there to personally accuse Goody Garlick), Goody Garlick was found innocent of all charges. Huzzah! The neighbors rallied around her. We knew you were innocent!, one might imagine them saying. We knew it all along! They returned to East Hampton and resumed their lives.

Both Joshua and Elizabeth Garlick continued working for Lion Gardiner. They had prosperity and success for the rest of their lives. In fact, both lived to be over ninety years old.

But what about Goody Davis, Goody Garlick's chief accuser? Did she continue complaining about Goody Garlick?

No, she did not last long enough to create more trouble. Goody Davis mysteriously died shortly after the Hartford trial.

Now, nobody here believes in witches ... do they?

The Capture Of Major John Andre
Lithograph by J. Baillie, 1845. (PD-1923)
It is said that when Major Andre was captured, plans for the taking of
West Point were found tucked in his stockings.

22

The Ghosts of Raynham Hall

TOWNSEND'S.

Woodcut of the home of Samuel Townsend in Oyster Bay, New York
(1852, *Pictorial Field Book of the Revolution* by Benson J Lossing)
(PD-1923)

In 1740, Samuel and Sarah Townsend, descendents of the British Townsends of Raynham Hall, bought six acres in Oyster Bay, New York and built a small but well-appointed home, naming it Raynham Hall after their ancestral history. "Raynham" means "River Home", and although the Oyster Bay location was not on a river, it was fairly close to Oyster Bay Cove – which also meant, during the American Revolution, it was quite near the British fleet that was sitting in New York Harbor and along Long Island Sound, just watching and waiting.

Samuel Townsend was prosperous and well-known. A Quaker statesman, he served as town clerk, justice of the peace and elected to the NY Provincial Congress in 1776. The Townsends had several children, including a son, Robert; and if his name sounds familiar, it is because he is the same Robert Townsend who was mentioned in a previous story! - Culper, Junior! One of General George Washington's spies!

General George Washington needed to get information about the British, but it was truly difficult for him to get the information he needed. Robert Townsend was one of the people who were able to help him. As a reporter for a British newspaper, Townsend would gain intelligence in Manhattan and pass it on through the spy ring to advise General Washington, and it enabled Washington to make decisions about troop movements and strategy. But at least one time, Townsend needed to get word to General Washington from something that happened not in the city, but right at his very own home.

The British invaded Long Island, securing the best homes and farms "in the name of the King," and homeowners were helpless to do anything about it. One surrendered their house and crops, or risk being accused of treason, tried and hanged. Raynham Hall, being in the very favorable location of Oyster Bay and owned by Quakers – who claimed they would just as well bury a British soldier as an American, they were both children of God – was a warm, comfortable and desirable location indeed. It quickly became the headquarters of Major John Andre, an outstanding British officer, fiercely determined to win the war with the Americans. Major Andre was pleased with the accommodations at Raynham Hall, and his troops were quartered on a hill nearby, under the command of Lt. Colonel John Graves Simcoe.

Lt. Colonel Simcoe became enamored with one of the Townsend daughters, a lovely young lady with long honey-colored hair. Her name was Sarah, but everyone called her Sally. The young officer quickly became a frequent visitor at Raynham Hall. In fact, Lt. Col. John Graves Simcoe was so smitten with Sally that he sent her a Valentine professing his admiration – the very first documented Valentine ever sent and received in the United States.

One morning Sally Townsend was quietly polishing the silver in the dining room of the house, using the eastern light to help her with her task in the dark room. She listened, half-attentively, to the quiet conversation occurring between John Simcoe and Major Andre in the kitchen. Suddenly she put down the spoon she was polishing and perked up her ears. What was this? She overheard the two men talking quietly and quite seriously about a plan to pay a great deal of money to an American captain, Benedict Arnold, to surrender his troops to the

Benedict Arnold, 1741-1801
From a painting by John Trumbull; print, 1894
(Courtesy Library of Congress, LC-USZ62-68483)

British at West Point. Sally did not know how important the information would be, but she knew that it was a very serious thing to be talking about such a terrible crime. Sick at heart, she tiptoed out of the room, and raced to find her brother Robert, who immediately passed the information to General George Washington. Upon receiving this intelligence, Washington furiously took troops and headed up the Hudson River to West Point immediately.

Because of Sally Townsend's courageous act and her brother Robert's immediate action, Major John Andre was quickly captured by the local American troops and hanged; some people say he was hung right there on the big oak tree in the front of the Raynham property (in actuality, he was tried and then hung at Tappan, New York). Benedict Arnold, learning of the failed plan, escaped from West Point and went down the Hudson River where he got on a British sloop-of-war, (ironically called "The Vulture"), and changed sides to the British. To this day we refer to someone who changes sides in a battle a traitor, a "turncoat", or even a "Benedict Arnold".

Lt. Col. John Graves Simcoe reportedly returned to England, leaving the brave Sally Townsend with nothing except a faded Valentine and a broken heart.

The old house was bought and sold a number of times, and additions were put on the house, including an entire wing in the middle 1800's.

Raynham Hall today is a bit like a time capsule, a small early colonial saltbox in front and an elegant Victorian manse in the back, connected by a central hallway, a staircase and a number of Victorian rooms that to us today look more haunted than the ones in the simple front of the house.

But it is indeed the section of the house that was present during all of these happenings in the Revolutionary War that is supposedly haunted. A number of ghosts have been reportedly seen in Raynham Hall. One tale tells of an overnight guest who once awoke to hear the snort and whinny of a horse outside her window. Looking out, she gasped in horror when she saw a ghostly white horse and rider, standing completely still on the lawn. He was dressed in a British officer's uniform, pale and transparent in the moonlight. It was believed to be none other than the ghost of Major John Andre.

Throughout the house have been reported cold spots, the smell of apples and cinnamon in the pantry, the smell of roses in the gallery in the back of the house that was once the kitchen. A mysterious workman once appeared at the door, and then completely disappeared.

Old Samuel Thompson has been sighted many times throughout the house, most often observed walking slowly up the stairs, leaning painfully on the railing. But the most famous ghost in Raynham Hall is the ghost of Sally

Townsend, who walks back and forth in the hall upstairs and haunts the children's chamber. Visitors have reported Sally's ghost watching them from the hall. Others have heard Sally angrily shushing them from the center of the room if they talk too loudly. Many believe that even years after the Revolutionary War ended, Sally spent much time in the children's nursery, sitting in a chair and rocking back and forth, looking out the window for her missing, beloved John Graves Simcoe. Broken and distraught, she never stopped lamenting the loss of her beloved, and not having children of her own. She never married. Although she reportedly died of a broken heart, she actually lived to be eighty years old.

Perhaps even in death, Sally Townsend still believes that one day, her Valentine, Lt. Col. John Graves Simcoe, will return once again to Raynham Hall... and she will still be there, like a faded valentine herself, waiting for him when he returns.

Eastern Screech Owl, Red Phase (Photo by Greg Hume)

23
The Hermitage of the Red Owl

It was the winter of 1877, and Charles and Emily Codman were settling in for the night. The Codmans were one of the founding families of "Modern Times", the idyllic community established in 1851 in what later became Brentwood. The community had dissolved, but the couple stayed; it was still a lovely place to live, despite a few oddballs who occasionally still came and went, and they were well respected by their neighbors.

The night was bitterly cold, with a winter storm already blowing snow and ice through the cracks and crevices of the house.

As Charles Codman closed the shutters of his home against the storm, he noticed a little red screech owl, perched on a branch and shivering in the wind and cold. The plight of the poor bird was not lost on the kindly man, but he knew that the bird, being a wild creature, would not come to him, even for shelter from the storm.

Suddenly the bird looked directly at Codman with its enormous eyes – and spoke aloud!

"Thou wouldst be kind to me?" it asked.

Too astounded to speak, Codman just nodded. The bird repeated:

"Thou wouldst be kind to me?"

Codman opened the shutters and bid the bird to enter. To his amazement, the bird hopped inside the window sill, then onto a table inside the room. The owl looked around, apparently making certain of his surroundings, and then, inexplicably, hopped up Codman's arm and onto his shoulder.

Scarcely breathing, Charles Codman brought the little red owl to his wife in the kitchen. Surprised, she immediately did what any woman would do for a visitor in the day, human or avian – she put out a small dish of water, and some corn for the bird to eat.

"I enjoy my corn roasted", the bird said.

What?

What would you have done if a talking owl said that to you? Probably just what Emily Codman did. Her mouth dropped open in amazement, and she dutifully began to roast the kernels of corn over the fire.

"Salt too, please" the owl continued. The flabbergasted couple just looked at each other. Emily found the old shaker, and shook salt over the corn. With that, the bird hopped off Charles' shoulder, onto the table and began to pick at the roasted, salted corn. The couple watched with mouths agape.

Shortly the bird was satisfied. It looked from one astounded face to the other, and spoke again.

"Many thanks, and blessings on this house" the bird said. "Shall I tell you my story?"

The Codmans just dumbly nodded.

The little red owl stretched its wings and

sighed, and told the Codmans an incredible tale. He claimed that many, many days and nights ago, he was once a man like they, the last of a great Indian tribe. He said his name was Oriwos. He told the couple that his tribe once fought a great battle on the Codman's land, where he was slain and left unburied. The owl continued his sad story, claiming that his unburied bones were there still, in a ravine close to the Codman's house. As long as his bones were not properly buried, the little red owl concluded, he was doomed to wander the earth and his soul would find no peace.

"How shall I comfort you?" asked Charles Codman.

"Find my bones. Bury them. Then I can rest" said the red owl. And to the astonishment of the Codmans, the bird simply disappeared.

The storm passed, and a few days later, after the snow had melted, Charles Codman went to the spot the owl said. Although he had passed the ravine hundreds of times before, he had never looked very closely. After a little while of searching, Charles Codman suddenly gasped. There, at his feet, was a human skull!

Codman carefully cleared the mud away and uncovered the skeleton. Gently he took the bones and wrapped them in a white cloth he had brought with him. He looked around, and seeing a particularly favorable spot under a grove of pine trees a little distance away, he thought it would be a good place to lay the

Indian brave to rest. Codman slowly dug out a grave and carefully placed the bones in the ground. Then he covered it over with dirt and stones, said a prayer over the grave, and with that gave Oriwos a decent burial.

Charles and Emily Codman spoke no more of the strange occurrence, but three days later, the owl reappeared on the same branch he was originally seen. Codman opened the shutter, and the owl hopped right into the room.

"You have treated me kindly and kept your word", the red owl said. "You will be sheltered from all adversity, and you will be the most respected of men. Draw my image and keep my picture close. I will watch over you and protect you always"

With that, the little red owl disappeared.

Charles Codman, unwilling to ever forget the astonishing creature, immediately picked up paper and pencil and drew a picture of the red owl, putting the little drawn image on his wall by the fireplace mantle.

From that day forward, Charles and Emily Codman called their home "The Hermitage of the Red Owl". True to the owl's prophecy, the Codman's home became the center of Brentwood society for the next decade. When his wife eventually died, Charles Codman put her ashes in an urn and kept it on the mantle next to the picture of the owl.

Charles Codman outlived his wife by a number of years; he was never alone, as he enjoyed the love and respect of family, neighbors and friends for the rest of his life. Upon his death, per his final instructions, his wife's ashes, and the little drawn picture of the amazing red owl, were buried with him in Brentwood Cemetery.

Portrait of a man-bat ("*Vespertilio-homo*"), from an edition of the Moon series published in Naples (PD-1923)

24
Man-Bats on the Moon!

In the year 1835, Long Islanders learned that there was life on the moon.

The news was right there on the front page of the August 26th edition of *The Hempstead Inquirer*, Long Island's foremost newspaper. *The Inquirer* got its information from the *New York Sun,* New York's foremost newspaper of the day.

It was during the final week of August 1835 that a long article appeared in serial form on the front page of the *New York Sun*. It bore the headline:

GREAT ASTRONOMICAL DISCOVERIES
LATELY MADE
BY SIR JOHN HERSCHEL, L.L.D. F.R.S. &c.
At the Cape of Good Hope
[From Supplement to the Edinburgh Journal of Science]

The famous British astronomer, Sir John Herschel, had gone to Cape Town in South Africa the year before, in 1834, and set up an observatory with a telescope of astonishing size – the lens was an astounding 25 feet across.

Herschel, the article declared, had established a "new theory of cometary phenomena"; he had discovered planets in other solar systems; and he had "solved or corrected nearly every leading problem of mathematical astronomy." Then the article revealed Herschel's final, stunning achievement: he had discovered life on the moon!

The article continued on and offered an elaborate account of the fantastic sights viewed by Herschel during his telescopic observation of the moon. It described a lunar topography that included vast forests, inland seas, and lilac-hued quartz pyramids. Readers learned that herds of bison wandered across the plains of the moon; that blue unicorns perched on its hilltops. Spherical, amphibious creatures rolled across its beaches to get from one place to another. Another day, Herschel apparently trained his telescope on another part of the moon and saw hut-dwelling, fire-wielding biped beavers that walked upright like a man and carried wood to their huts. But on yet another day, Herschel saw the man-bats. These were a race of winged humans living in pastoral harmony around a mysterious, golden-roofed temple. Herschel dubbed these latter creatures the *Vespertilio-homo,* or "man-bat".

The Sun reached a circulation of 15,000 daily on the first of the stories. When the discovery of the man-bats on the moon appeared, the *Sun* possessed the largest circulation of any newspaper in the world: 19,360.

The world went wild. People cried and prayed. A Springfield, Massachusetts,

Illustration of "The Ruby Amphitheater"
from the *New York Sun*, August 28, 1835
(Courtesy Library Of Congress LC-DIG-pga-02667)

missionary society resolved to send missionaries
to the moon to convert and civilize the bat men.

Rival editors were frantic. Many of them
pretended to have access to the original articles
and began reprinting the *Sun*'s series. Edgar
Allan Poe himself, about to publish one of his
stories, pulled it from the paper, saying that
there was nothing he could write that would top
this.

After six days of the fantastic series, the
authors announced that the observations had
been terminated by the destruction of the
enormous telescope, by means of the sun
causing the lens to act as a "burning glass," and
(conveniently) setting fire to the observatory.

Amazingly, very few people doubted the stories. Then within a few days, very few people believed them! Eventually it was said to be a hoax, and it was finally revealed that Herschel never wrote the stories. Not even his travelling companion and stenographer, Dr. Andrew Grant, who was supposedly with Herschel in South Africa, wrote them (in fact, Dr. Andrew Grant was fictitious as well.) No, nobody ever owned up to the elaborate scheme, but it became widely suspected that the author was a newspaperman by the name of Richard A. Locke, who was working for the *New York Sun* in the summer of 1835.

Richard Adams Locke (Courtesy Edgar Allen Poe Society of Baltimore)

Locke was – as it turned out – an astonishingly good liar. He had a serious, scientific demeanor, and his piercing eyes and prominent forehead gave him the appearance of an academic. His very career as a writer was a result of uncontested near-truths – to make himself appear more intellectual and thus employable, for example, he claimed that he studied at Cambridge. (In fact, he was told to attend Cambridge by his father, but he apparently never attended, much less graduated). There is, however, no doubt that he was creative and highly intelligent; Locke was particularly well-versed in history and the sciences, and had more than a passing interest in astronomy.

Was Locke really the author of the amazing story, or was it just another of his lies? It was such an extraordinarily good hoax, with its unknown author taking every pain to give the appearance of veracity, that no one was really completely sure. Even the tiniest facts were quite believable. Not even the most astute of scientists were aware that there was no such publication as the Edinburgh Journal of Science!

But here's the strangest thing, as my friend Henry pointed out –

Several years later, in 1897, the *New York Sun* became famous for running a response to a letter from a little girl who was asking about the existence of Santa Claus. The editorial, entitled

"Yes, Virginia, there IS a Santa Claus", proved for once and for all that the *New York Sun* only prints the truth.

So therefore, Henry told me, he, for one, firmly believes there *are* man-bats on the moon.

The Inhabitants of the Moon, 1836. The story literally "went viral" in its day. This lunar landscape is a depiction from the Welsh edition of the story. (PD-1923)

25
The Most Haunted Road on Long Island

Just southwest of Huntington is West Hills, best known as the birthplace of the poet Walt Whitman. Bordered on the west by Woodbury and on the north by Cold Spring Harbor, it is a beautiful, treed area, home to Jayne's Hill, the highest elevation on Long Island, and boasts many horse farms and natural springs. In the middle of all of this beauty, however, is an ominous path, about a mile long. It is dark and strange and mysterious. Its name is Sweet Hollow Road.

Sweet Hollow Road is the most haunted road on Long Island. Some people think nearby Mount Misery Road is the most haunted, but it's not. You'd think that because of its name – Mount Misery. However, it is called that because in the days of horses and wagons, whenever it rained it became impossible for the carts and wagons to make way through the mud. Local folks called the road "Mount Misery" because it was a misery trying to get a wagon through.

No, Sweet Hollow Road is haunted by not one, not two – but five different spirits!

The thoroughfare is the home to The Lady in White. She is sometimes seen walking quietly along the side of the road. If you pass her and then stop, perhaps to offer her a ride (as it is not a very safe place to be walking alone in the dark on the side of a narrow road, even if she is wearing white) when you turn around to look back at her, she will have vanished into thin air. On certain nights, at the witching hour, she has been known to throw herself in front of oncoming vehicles. (The witching hour is not midnight, as many people think. It's three o'clock in the morning. Trust me... if you're driving up Sweet Hollow Road at three o'clock in the morning, you deserve what you get. Three o'clock in the morning is no time to be on Sweet Hollow Road.) When you jump out of your wagon to see what you have hit, nothing, nothing will be there!

Now, if you don't see the Lady in White, you might be pulled over by a policeman. Do not stop for the policeman! Don't even look at him! It is said that the policeman will pull over a vehicle and ask for your papers. But when he turns around – he is missing the back of his head! If a policeman wants you to pull over on Sweet Hollow Road, do not stop until you get to a well-lit spot at the end of the road!

There is a bridge that passes over Sweet Hollow Road. A nearly hundred year old legend claims that late at night, the ghost of a suicide victim can be seen, hanging there by a rope and swaying, back and forth, beneath the bridge. It is said one can summon the ghost by stopping your carriage, extinguishing all lights, and honking your horn three times. And you will see the ghost of a boy hanging by his neck off the bridge!

And still the horror continues! At one point, there is a cemetery along the side of Sweet Hollow Road. Corpse lights have been seen in that cemetery. You know what corpse lights are, don't you? Sometimes they are called will o'the wisp. Also, corpse candles. Whatever you want to call them, they are little balls of light that float in the distance, and try to get you to follow them. Do not follow them! People who follow corpse lights are rarely seen again.

And finally, in the woods along the side of Sweet Hollow Road, people have reported seeing a Hound from Hell. Reports claim that this apparition is an enormous black dog with huge jaws and red-glowing eyes, snorting fire from its nostrils. It disappears from one place and reappears in another. If you see it and it howls, it means someone close to you will die soon. If you see the Hound from Hell, don't follow it! Don't go near it! A number of people over the past three hundred years have gone in search of the dog – and were never seen again.

But so many people have travelled up and down Sweet Hollow Road, and I have never seen them again...so the stories of the spirits must be true. However, I don't want to spend any more time there than I need to. And trust me - neither do you!

Root Cellar, Peace and Plenty Inn (Author's own photo)

Epilogue

If you should find yourself lost in the dark on Sweet Hollow Road, whatever you do, please, please do not try to find refuge at the Peace and Plenty Inn! Whatever you do! Because the old, dark and foreboding building, just off Sweet Hollow Road, the charmingly-named Peace and Plenty Inn... is haunted as well!

How did I find out about it? Oh... the very worst possible way. But that will keep for another day!

I hope you enjoyed my stories. Perhaps you might tell them to others!

I leave you now in good blessings – and I bid you peace.

Illustration from *'Grist Wind-mills at East Hampton,'*
Picturesque America, New York, 1872. by John Karst
(LOC-HAER NY,52-HAMTE,2--34)

Bibliography and Resources

1. *A Fleeting Moment in History: Modern Times* by Verne Dyson (1964, Brentwood Public Library, Brentwood, New York)

2. *Anecdotes and Events in Long Island History* by Verne Dyson (1969, Ira J. Friedman, Inc., Port Washington, New York)

3. *Antiquities of Long Island* by Gabriel Furman (published originally 1874; reissued 1968 by Ira J. Friedman, Inc., Port Washington, New York)

4. *Colonial Long Island Folklife* by John H. Braunlein (1976, Museums at Stony Brook, Stony Brook, New York)

5. *Discovering the Past: Writings of Jeannette Edwards Rattray 1893-1974 Relating to the History of the Town of East Hampton* (The East Hampton Historical Collection)

6. *Heather Flower and Other Indian Tales of Long Island* by Verne Dyson (1969; Ira J. Friedman, Inc., Port Washington, New York)

7. *Historical Collections of the State of New York* by John W. Barber and Henry Howe (originally published 1841; reissued 1970 by Ira J. Friedman, Inc., Port Washington, New York)

8. *Home Town Long Island : the History of Every Community on Long Island in Stories*

and Photographs (1999, Newsday Inc.,
Melville, New York)

9. *Long Island Before the Revolution: A
   Colonial Study* (1896; originally published
   as *Early Long Island*) by Martha Bochee
   Flint. (1967; Ira J. Friedman, Inc., Port
   Washington, New York)

10. Long Island Genealogy:
    www.longislandgenealogy.com. Online
    resources of diverse historical background,
    books and ephemera.

11. *Myths and Legends of our Own Land,* by
    Charles M. Skinner, (1896; J.B. Lippincott
    Company, Philadelphia and London,)

12. Project Guttenberg, *www.gutenberg.org*.
    Excellent resource for obscure texts and
    books; through their efforts many ancient
    sources are now available online for
    educators, students and readers.

13. *Sound Rising: Long Island Sound at the
    Forefront of America's Struggle for
    Independence* by Richard Radune (2011;
    Research in Time Publications.)

14. *Stories of Old Long Island* by Birdsall
    Jackson (originally published 1934;
    reissued 1968 by Ira J. Friedman, Inc., Port
    Washington, New York)

15. *The Diary of Mary Cooper: Life on a Long
    Island Farm, 1768-1773* (1981, Oyster Bay
    Historical Society)

16. *The Empire State: A Compendious History of the Commonwealth of New York* by Benson J. Lossing, L.L.D. (1888, American Publishing Company, Hartford, Connecticut)

17. *The Fabled Past: Tales of Long Island* by Edith Hay Wychoff (1970, Kennikat Press, Port Washington, New York)

18. *The Human Story of Long Island* by Verne Dyson (1969; Ira J. Friedman, Inc., Port Washington, New York)

19. *The Huntington Common: The Village Green* by the Huntington Historical Society (1976, Huntington, New York)

20. *The Indian Place Names on Long Island and Islands Adjacent* by William W. Tooker (1911; G.P. Putnam and Sons, New York and London, The Knickerbocker Press)

21. *The Montaukett Indians of Eastern Long Island* by John A. Strong (2006, Syracuse University Press, New York)

22. *The Thirteen Tribes of Long Island* by Paul Bailey (originally pub. 1959; reissued 1982 by Friends for Long Island Heritage)

23. *The Pirates' Own Book*: *Authentic Narratives of the Most Celebrated Sea Robbers* by Charles Elms (original publication 1837; reprinted 1924, Marine Research Society, Salem, Massachusetts)

24. *The Window to the Street* by Harriet Valentine (1981, Cold Spring Harbor

Whaling Museum, Cold Spring Harbor,
New York)

25. *Twenty-One Choice Stories of Long Island*
(1988, Friends for Long Island's Heritage,
Muttontown, New York)

26. *Witches, Whales, Petticoats and Sails:
Adventures and Misadventures of Long
Island History* by Barbara Marhoefer (1971,
Ira J. Friedman Division of Kennikat Press,
Port Washington, New York)

Appendix A:

How to find out more...
and a few of my favorites.

Fairly comprehensive listings of the vast number of museums and historical societies on Long Island can be found online through a variety of websites, including Visit Historic Long Island.com, LongIsland.com, and both the Nassau County and Suffolk County government websites.

Most town libraries have a local history department, and a helpful staff person who is extremely knowledgeable about the subject. Just go on in and ask!

The majority of the older towns have dedicated historical societies, and many are housed in fascinating, significant buildings in their own right. At the moment, I am thinking of Southampton, East Hampton, Oyster Bay, Huntington and the Three Village Historical Society. But there are many more! Take a look!

There are museums on Long Island dedicated to their obvious historic focus (The American Airpower Museum in Farmingdale, for example), but others that have obscure titles and are yet just as relevant to understanding Long Island's history (like the oddly-named Second House Museum in Montauk). There are also museums dedicated to individuals and groups who made a significant contribution to Long Island – African Americans, Native Americans, firefighters, whalers, scientists, artists, poets, writers, performers, industrial tycoons; there are even museums dedicated to telephone pioneers, guitars and shorthand! If you have a particular interest – just look it up! There is likely a museum dedicated to it.

None of the museums or societies above or in the following eight museums discussed below has asked me to mention them – in fact, they do not even know that I have! But everyone has their own favorite places, of course. Since you asked (and even if you didn't), in no particular order, here are a few of my absolute favorites:

<u>Raynham Hall Museum</u> – This tiny Oyster Bay home, featured in two of my stories, is something of a duel-era time capsule. The original pre-Revolutionary saltbox house is from the mid 1700's, and its extension from the 1800's is interpreted in all of the fringe, wall coverings and excess one imagines the Victorian era to be. It is essentially two museums in one, and its dedication to the small details in both eras is a treat. Definitely worth a visit.

<u>Old Bethpage Village Restoration</u> – This Nassau County-owned facility is the only actually *restored* village on the entire East Coast – and with competition from places like Colonial

Williamsburg, Old Sturbridge Village, Mystic Seaport, and Plimouth Plantation, that is saying a lot. Despite the funding issues most county governments face, the houses seen here have persevered, largely because of the dedication of staff and volunteers. What makes Old Bethpage special is that each of the historic buildings came from a part of Long Island and were moved, some timber by timber, others as an intact structure, to the Village in the 1970's. With its general stores (there are actually two of them), blacksmith shop, hat shop, church, one-room schoolhouse and farms, Old Bethpage gives a visitor an up-close and first-hand look at the way people in the 19th Century lived and worked (although distances between buildings are a lot closer than they would have been two hundred years ago). Bring a picnic lunch and step back in time.

Old Westbury Gardens – The former home of American lawyer and businessman John S. Phipps, his wife Margarita Grace Phipps (heiress to the Grace Shipping Lines) and their four children (and pets), this 200-acre property boasts some of the most magnificent landscaped gardens in the world. On a hill overlooking several reflecting ponds, an adorable Tudor-style playhouse for the children, the splendid horticulture and acres of woodlands, stands the Phipps' elegant Charles II-style mansion. Built in 1906, it is breathtakingly lush and luxurious, yet still manages to maintain an aura of graceful accessibility, with an obvious love for family, dogs, children and friends. That elegant combination of upper-class grace and yet wholesome family fun is echoed in the next two of my favorites:

Sagamore Hill - The former home of President Theodore Roosevelt, this beautiful mansion and estate in Oyster Bay Cove is owned and maintained by the National Park Service, and is a testament to President Roosevelt's love of family, friends, animals, preservation and natural beauty. One can only imagine what it must have been like to sit on the sprawling west porch, watching the sunset over Oyster Bay Cove (huge trees now obscure some of the view, but it is still stunning), lemonade in hand, listening to Mr. Roosevelt expound on his vision for America.

The Bayard-Cutting Arboretum – The former home of attorney and financier William Bayard Cutting, the enormous property (originally one thousand acres), including its 1886 mansion, farm and fields on the Connetquot River, is now owned and maintained by New York State Parks, Recreation and Historic Preservation. Its huge wrap-around porch and sprawling lawn features wooden Adirondack chairs for visitors to sit and relax and perhaps sip a purchased cup of tea. This is one house and property where most visitors seem to feel immediately comfortable, and are able to imagine that this is actually their home – at least for a few hours.

Walt Whitman Birthplace State Historic Site - This humble home, built in 1819 by poet Walt Whitman's father, and where Whitman himself was born, has dedicated itself to furthering not only poetry, but all literacy. The actual operations and events are run by the Walt Whitman Birthplace Association, a small group of extremely dedicated individuals who work hard to develop and promote interesting literacy-based programs. Nearly every month they sponsor events featuring prominent authors and outstanding poets, and offer yearly writing contests for children, and educational programs for all ages.

Sagtikos Manor – This pre-Revolutionary War estate in Bay Shore, built in 1697, was home to generations of renowned New York families whose names live on all over the Island: Van Cortlandt, Carll, Thompson, Gardiner. This beautiful mansion was the headquarters for the British army for a short time during the Revolution, but was a documented stopping-place for our first American President when he toured Long Island in 1790 to thank his troops. Yes, George Washington actually slept here!

The Cradle of Aviation Museum – Near the

actual site where Charles Lindbergh took off for his historic flight from Roosevelt Field to Paris in 1927, the museum originally consisted of a collection of Long Island aircraft housed in an old aircraft hangar. Over time, the museum developed from these humble beginning into a world-class site dedicated to preserving Long Island's aerospace heritage. The museum offers an IMAX theater and popular exhibits and programs, but, to me, the undisputed "star" of the museum is the brilliant gold, silver and black thermal-shielded Grumman Lunar Module. It was the predecessor of this LM-13 – the LM-5 "Eagle" – that safely and successfully landed men on the moon in 1969. The LM and its associated exhibit is, in my opinion, even more awe-inspiring than its counterpart in the Smithsonian Air and Space Museum in Washington, D.C., and it alone is worth the visit.

Acknowledgements:

I would like to thank Jim McKenna, Ken Balcom, Kenneth Quinn and Henry Clark for the opportunities and assistance they gave me since we first met at Old Bethpage Village Restoration a number of years ago. Their dedication was an inspiration to me, and these four men never failed to support me in my storytelling research, answering thousands of questions over the years. Henry's inspired lunacy was a particular joy, and I am delighted to know that a new generation of middle readers will be treated to his enormous and humorous writing talents. Henry, the Man-Bats are for you!

I would also like to thank my readers: Marilyn Johnson, M.A., Ed.D. and Cynthia Serafin-Maus, M.A.. Their insights and kind comments – and even kinder and gentler criticisms – made this a better book.

I would also be remiss if I did not mention the many libraries and local history librarians whose interest and dedication assisted me greatly. I would like to make particular mention of the good people at the East Hampton Public Library, the Bay Shore-Brightwaters Public Library, the Brentwood Public Library, and especially the South Huntington Public Library for all of their help and support.

The literally hundreds of audiences – school

groups, Life-Long Learners, library patrons, associations and historical societies – I have had the privilege of entertaining over the years have been a great source of story input, re-imagining and editing. Perhaps they thought that I was providing a service to them, when in fact they were providing an invaluable service to me!

I want to thank my sons, Christopher and Timothy - both historians and educators - whose love and dedication to their crafts and their interpretations inspire me daily. Finally, my deepest thanks to my husband Tom, whose support of me is boundless, and who never complains about having to go out and pick up pizza for dinner yet again.

About the Author

Janet Emily Demarest was born and raised on Long Island. She holds an MBA from Adelphi University in Organizational Behavior, and an Advanced Certificate in Creative Writing from SUNY/ Stony Brook in Southampton. She also completed research and coursework in American Maritime History at the Frank C. Munson Institute in Mystic Seaport, Connecticut.

Trading on her extensive group and classroom skills, she tours, lectures and performs her own written works, including *Things That* Went *Bump in the Night;* and *Women in Long Island Legend: The Trollop, the Witch and the Brokenhearted.* Many of the obscure stories, local legends and lore gathered for her programs form the basis for *Tales from the General Store.*

The author is an educator, playwright, actor and artist, and the Storyteller-in-Residence at Old Bethpage Village Restoration. She is a proud member of The Dramatists Guild of America, The Authors Guild, and the New York Folklore Society.

All pictures in this book listed as "public domain" are so designated because the work is in the public domain in the United States, and those countries with a copyright term of life of the author plus 100 years or less, and/or because it was published (or registered with the U.S. Copyright Office) before January 1, 1923.

All uncredited photographs were taken by the author.

33728150R00115

Made in the USA
Charleston, SC
22 September 2014